THE OTHER SIDE OF LIFE

Marjorie B. Thompson

Kendall/Hunt
Publishing Company

A   403499   01

This book is dedicated to the spirit guide who conveyed to me the lessons contained herein; and
To the many individuals here on the earth plane who have encouraged my efforts to bring this book to fruition, and
To Jim Conlon.

Contents

Preface

The book which you are about to read has been dictated to me, through automatic writing, by someone, in spirit.

As a Spiritualist medium, I work closely each day with those in spirit and to have someone dictate a book to me as I sat at my typewriter was no more of a feat than getting messages from spirit for the benefit of those who come to me seeking help.

The Other Side of Life takes you beyond the veil that separates this earthly plane and the plane which exists just beyond the reach of our five senses. It has been written to give you more knowledge of what to expect when you reach that time when you are ready to leave your Earthly plane and journey to your new home.

The spirit author has tried to show you what life is like on the other side, in a language which is very simple, and down-to-earth, so that all may understand.

You are also given a series of lessons to help you live a better life while you are still in the physical body, and, thus, to prepare yourself for a better life over there.

You will find, lessons that help you understand how communication with spirit is done, and how such communication can help you in your everyday life.

This is not the first time that a book has been dictated by spirit to a medium here on Earth, nor will it be the last. There is much that needs to be told, and if individuals will not listen to their own guides, it becomes necessary for spirit to put the information together in the form of a book so that people may be reached.

Consider yourself fortunate if you have been led to pick up this particular book for, when you have finished reading it, you will have been made aware that you can communicate with your own guides in spirit and, therefore, open yourself up to all the help that spirit can give you. You will understand also that one need not fear "death", for it is only a move to another location, a new place of residence.

Use this book as a guideline in your daily living, and you will find that your life takes on new meaning, new hope, for there is still time.

Now, turn the page and step into *The Other Side of Life.*

—Marjorie B. Thompson
P.O. Box 868
Southington, CT. 06489

Chapter I
THE BEGINNING

Now we are to begin a journey into the realm of the unknown. There are many questions to be answered and many things to be talked about to clear up the doubt and the mystery that surrounds the "other side of life". For those of us who have already made the transition, there is no mystery. Only an unfolding of new and exciting experiences each day. We are here now to tell you who have not yet made the transition a little about our life here.

We, who have passed on, are fully aware of everything that goes on around us. We are not dead. We have only made a change in our residence, so to speak, and now dwell in another part of the universe, a part which cannot be seen by the physical eye. We, however, can see you who are still in the physical body and, if we have a mind to do so, can be aware of everything that takes place on your side of life. We say, "if we have a mind to" because we are usually very busy here, and we do not keep our eye on you every minute of the day. There is no need to interfere in anyone's private life, and, therefore, unless there is a specific reason for our being interested in the life of one particular person, or a group of people, we do not tune in. It would be unthinkable for one of us to pry into someone's life, unless we had been called upon to help with some particular problem. We never interfere just for the sake of having something to do. On the contrary, we have much to do here on the other side of life.

When I first arrived here, I was very apprehensive, and a bit puzzled. I could not understand how it was that I was able to be aware of everything around me, and yet not be a physical being, as I had been prior to my "death". I was able to see and to hear and to think and to move about. Actually, I was able to move about more easily than I had previously

1

because now I was no longer bound by the physical body which I had carried around for so long. My sense of hearing and my sight seemed to be so much more acute now, that I could hear even very distant sounds and see things at a great distance.

There was, at first, nothing around me. I seemed to be floating in the midst of a gray cloud or mist. However, after what seemed to be a very short time, I was aware of other figures and shapes around me and it seemed as though the mist was becoming thinner, so that I was able to see a dim light very far away. I turned and began to move toward the light and as I did so, the figures around me also began to move, and I sensed that they were motioning me on, toward the source of light. I felt, then, a feeling of lightness within me, and the apprehension that I had felt previously soon disappeared. I knew now that I was not alone.

As we moved out of the mist, the light became so bright, and so warm, that I thought a thousand suns were shining on me. I could not tell where the source of light was, for it seemed to be all around me. I continued to move forward, and now, as I looked about me, I was aware of people everywhere. Some of them I thought I knew, although I was not quite able to make out their faces. Others, I was sure I had not known before, and yet, there was a feeling of warmth and love from them which made me feel as though I somehow belonged there with them. I continued to move along in the direction I had been going and as I did so, I realized that the light which had been so brilliant, was no longer seen but that I was now in the midst of a beautiful garden, filled with flowers of every kind. There were familiar old favorites, and also there were flowers that I had never seen before, of such beauty and color that I am unable to describe them to you. Beyond The Garden there were green fields and hills with trees of every kind. I heard music and it seemed as though everywhere I looked there were birds and butterflies in the most brilliant colors and the most exotic shapes that I have ever seen. There was also a large tree, with a stream running beneath it. The water ran silvery and clear, and I could almost hear it singing as it made its way through the flower garden and disappeared from my sight.

Looking about me at all this beauty I wondered, "Is this Heaven?"

"You may call it that if you like, but we prefer to call it home," a voice said, and I turned to find that there was a young man standing beside me. I asked his name, but he said that was unimportant, and that he was here to guide me to the place I was to go in order that I could begin my progress and find out what it was that I had to do here, for, contrary to popular belief, one does not sleep, nor does one lie about all day doing nothing.

We moved along, out of The Garden, and I was again amazed at the wonderful feeling of lightness and the ease with which it is possible to move when you are not encumbered by the physical body. Wherever we went, there was beauty, and I could hear voices and laughter as we moved along, and sometimes music. I saw groups of children in the distance; some seemed to be studying or reading, while others romped and played on the lush green lawn.

"There is much to be done here," said my young guide. "When you are introduced to your Master, he will outline for you what is necessary for you to do in order that you may progress. Do not fear, however, for if you enter through The Garden, you have probably not had so bad a life that you would be bogged down here with problems and tasks which have carried over with you."

We moved on, and I was surprised to see before us a group of buildings, which appeared to be a school or a university, as I could see people coming and going, carrying books and papers in their arms. My young friend advised me that I was to enter by the main door, and once I was inside the building I would be shown the way to the Master's office. He told me that it was here, in this school, that the new arrivals were given their assignments and told a little of what to expect in their new home. I thanked him and had hardly gotten the words out of my mouth, when he was gone. I marveled again, at the speed with which one could move about here in this strange new place.

As I entered the building, a young woman greeted me and pointed to a door a short distance down the hallway, where she said I was to report. I moved quickly down the hall and, before I had even knocked on the door, it opened, and I went inside. Seated at a large desk before me was a man. His hair was white and one would expect to see someone very elderly, but when I looked at his face, I was startled to see such peacefulness and serenity there that I was not aware of any sign of age at all. I remembered then that everyone that I had met on my journey to this building had had that same peaceful, serene look upon their face. I realized, also, that I had felt serene and peaceful myself, since I had lost those feelings of apprehension which I had when I first came to this place.

He motioned to me to be seated and then began to glance through a set of papers which he had on his desk. Occasionally, he would glance at me and then go back to his reading again. I did not feel ill-at-ease, for there was such a feeling of love and warmth in that office that I would have been content to sit there forever.

As if he had read my thoughts, the gentleman smiled and said, "Soon one would grow very tired of having nothing to do, even in a place such as this. That is why we are assigned certain tasks which, as we complete them, help us to grow and to progress spiritually, so that we grow ever closer to the Father. Do not worry, for there will also be time for you to relax and to do whatever it is that you would like to do. And, there is much for you to see here in your new home."

He went on to tell me that I had progressed much in my spiritual growth, while I was still in the physical body, and this was why I had entered through The Garden. However, he said that there are many who have not progressed spiritually, and many who did not believe that there was anything more than the life which they had on earth, and these did not enter through The Garden, but came by way of many other paths, some of which were not very pleasant. I would, he said, learn more of this later.

We talked for some time, and I was given an outline of what I was to do, and then he told me that it was time now for me to begin my new life. We said good-by, and, before I left, he advised me that at any time that I had any questions or problems, he would be happy to help me with them. He also told me that once I left the building, I would never be alone, for there would always be someone to guide me and show me the way.

Chapter II
"LOVE YE, ONE ANOTHER"

There is much to be done here. However, one does not tire, but, rather, enjoys being a part of the busy, friendly community. One of the tasks I was given was to try to make those who are still on Earth understand that there is more to life than what they see there before them. That is only one side of life. Life here, on the other side, has much to offer, and it is while you are still in the physical body that you should prepare yourself for the journey you will take when you discard that body.

If you are a warm, loving, spiritual person while you are there on Earth, your transition to this life will be fairly simple, for you will come through The Garden, as I did. If, however, you are uncaring, selfish, dishonest, or have any of the other negative traits that human beings are wont to have, you must begin now to change your ways, for you never know when you will be called to the other side, and you cannot begin to "do better" tomorrow. There may be no tomorrow. For, we never know when it will be time for us to move on to the other life.

Have you thought about life after "death" as you call it? Do you believe that there is something more to look forward to, or only eternal sleep. What does "death" mean to you? Is it a frightening thing to look forward to? Would you rather not think of it at all? You must think about it, for you must begin, now, to prepare your way so that the transition will be smooth and easy for you when it is time for you to go. "And how am I to do that?" you ask. It is simple. Just listen. I will tell you how.

You must begin at the beginning, at the beginning of each day, for each day that is given you is the beginning of your life. It matters not what you have been, but only what you are from that moment on. It is never too late.

When you awaken in the morning, do you ever stop to think how wonderful it is that you were given another day of life? Do you begin your day with grumbling and moaning because you have to get up? Did you ever stop to think that you are fortunate to be able to get up? There are many, each day, who do not awaken, many who leave before they have a chance to begin their life anew. Thank God, for you have been given another day, another chance.

I speak of death as a "transition", for it is just that. It is merely making a move from one home to another. There should be nothing frightening about this. The thing that should concern you while you are on Earth, is how to prepare your future home, so that when you do make the move you will have something pleasant waiting for you and will not have to spend unnecessary time wandering around and searching for something that you are not ready for. If one has been living in poverty, spiritually speaking, one does not, or should not, expect to move into a mansion when the time comes for the crossing over to the other side. If you were to visit a beautiful home there on Earth, you would wash and dress and prepare yourself so that you would be acceptable and not be out of place. Well, the same is true for your new home. You must prepare yourself for the best by being the best you can be, while you are still in the body. Please note that I did not say that you should be better than everyone else, only the best that *you* can be. If you strive to give of yourself each day, and to do the best you can in whatever you have undertaken, then you are on the way to spiritual growth. The most important factor, however, is that you do these things without looking for a pat on the back, or a special award. Do them quietly, without fanfare, and even though you receive no thanks, know that you are paving the way so that you may enter your new home through The Garden. Be kind to others. Be gracious and giving. Try always to do a little extra, rather than doing only what has been assigned to you each day, and, perhaps, not even that. Do not try to see how much you can get away with, but rather how much you can give away, of your time, and your energy. Give, even though it be only a kind word, or a thoughtful gesture, to help someone else along the way. For, as you give, you also receive. You may not always be aware of any reward that is given to you for your efforts, for, many times, the rewards are not given on the Earth. You do, however, prepare the way to your new home. Each time you give of yourself, you are placing another signpost along the pathway so that when you arrive here you are not confused and bewildered, but can see in which direction you should go. These "signposts" I speak of are not actual signs. They are spirit beings who will welcome you and show you the way.

It is sometimes difficult when one first makes the transition, to see one's surroundings. It may seem that you are surrounded by a mist, or a fog. If you have done your work well, on Earth, then you need not fear, for the spirit beings who are to be your signposts, will be waiting for you when you cross over, and they will show you the way. Even though you may not "see" them at first, you will be aware of them around you by the warmth and the love they send out to newcomers when they welcome them home. Once your eyes have become adjusted to their new vision, you will be able to see your guides, and the mist will begin to disappear.

If you are prepared, crossing over is such a simple matter that you will wonder why you ever thought it would be anything less than that. If, however, you continue to go through life there on Earth constantly taking, and never giving, always trying to outsmart the other fellow, and, generally, being not much good to yourself or to anyone else, you will not find the transition so easy. Many people believe that when they make the crossing they "have it made". This is not so. For those of you who do not try to improve your life by being gentle, kind, and all of the other good things that make up a spiritual person, have many trials and lessons waiting to be learned when you reach this side. You can "undo" the mistakes you have made, and you can "make up" for things you have left undone there on Earth, but wouldn't it be better if you would just learn to live a more God-like life while you are there? Then, when you make the transition to this life, you will not have to waste time going back over things that should have been taken care of while you were in the body. True, you cannot be perfect, but you can be the best that you can be. That is all that is expected of you.

The more spiritual one becomes, while on Earth, the closer one becomes to God. Your spiritual growth determines at what level you will be when you reach this side of life. Some believe that they become spiritual by believing in God, or by believing in Jesus. These are good foundations for your spiritual progress, but they do not make you a highly spiritual person. Others believe that if they meditate they have become very spiritual. Here again, this is a good beginning, but you cannot sit in meditation all your life and expect to have fulfilled your mission there on Earth. There are many other factors that contribute to your spiritual growth.

A truly spiritual person does not shut himself off from others so that he may direct his thoughts to higher levels of consciousness. And, when I say he does not "shut himself off" I mean either by removing himself from the scene physically, emotionally, or mentally. For, there are many ways to remove oneself from the mainstream of life. To grow spiritually, you must be involved with life. You must care about those with whom you come in contact as you go through life. I hesitate to use the word "love" as so many of you have the wrong idea of the meaning of this word. Loving someone is nothing more than caring for them. To love those around you means only that you treat others as you would like to be treated yourself. There are many degrees of love. The love you give to your sweetheart or your mate; the love you give to your children; love given to friends; love given to pets. All of these feelings that you feel toward each of these is a different degree of love, but beneath it all is the feeling that you care for someone, or something. To give love to those you meet along the way, as you go through life, is only to show each one that someone cares for them, even if only for a passing moment. What a wonderful thing it is to know that someone cared for you, that someone reached out to touch you, or gave you a kind word.

It is so easy to push others aside. Some of you go through life as though you were playing football. You tuck your emotions under your arm, lower your head, and then charge through life looking neither right nor left, never noticing who it was that you pushed aside, and caring less; always trying to reach your goal, to make points for yourself. Ah! You've made it! But what do you have? There is still an emptiness within you, a feeling that something is still missing. Well, no matter, you'll charge for the goal at the other end of the field next time. Perhaps that is where it's at.

You fool! How many times have you run from one goal to another and still ended up with nothing. The feeling of emptiness and of something lacking still inside you? You can do this for the rest of your life and still find, when you reach the end of the road, that you have nothing. Wake up, before it is too late for you to change your ways. Lift up your head and look around you. There are people all about you, and if you but take a moment to notice someone and to give a little of yourself, you will find that the feeling of nothingness inside you begins to lessen and instead there is a feeling of accomplishment, and beauty and love. For, now, you begin to be important in the scheme of life and now your spirit begins to grow. Now the scoring in your game of life begins, for nothing you do for others goes unnoticed by those who are keeping track of your spiritual growth. As I mentioned earlier, we do not watch you every minute, but we are aware of those things which are important for us to know, and it is important that we are aware of the spiritual growth of each individual there on Earth. It is not important who you impress there on Earth, but what is important is the impression you make on those beings on the other side of life who are watching your progress and your spiritual growth.

The most important factor in your spiritual growth is your involvement with others, how you get along with your fellow man. Therefore, remember that you must always be a part of life. You cannot sit on the sidelines and watch it go by, thinking that because you are not involved you do no harm, and, therefore, you are very good and very God-like. You harm yourself when you do that. You must *participate*. Go among the people and give of yourself and though you are not a perfect being, you are at least trying, and that is what matters the most.

Chapter **III**
WHY ME?

I will discuss now another factor in spiritual development. I begin by asking you, "How have you handled your problems?" "My problems?" you say. "What has that to do with spiritual growth?"

Each problem, each adversity that has been placed in your path as you have gone through life has been put there for a reason. They were given to you as lessons which you were to learn. As you went through school, were you not given a new lesson each time you had completed the one before? And, if you did not learn the lesson, was it not given to you again? So it is in life. Some of you lament that you never seem to get anywhere—it seems as though you have the same problems over and over. "What is wrong?" Think back. How did you handle the problem the first time it was given to you? Did you try to make the best of the situation, and try to handle it to the best of your ability, knowing that there was a lesson there somewhere for you to learn, and trying to understand what that lesson was? Or did you avoid the situation as much as possible just hoping that eventually it would take care of itself and you would be done with it? You cannot take your problems and push them aside, or dump them in someone else's lap to be solved, and not expect to see them come into your life again, somewhere along the way. These lessons were given to you. *You* must learn to solve them for yourself, or, if there is no apparent solution, you must learn to handle them, to accept them and do the best you can with them. Each time you solve a problem, or learn to handle it, you are learning the lesson you were meant to learn from that particular situation. Can you feel, as you learn your lessons, something happening inside you? There is a difference in you. You feel stronger; there is a feeling of well-being within you that you cannot explain. Were someone to ask you why you feel this way, you could not begin to tell them. I can tell you why. It is because your spirit is growing. You have nourished it by the way in which you have handled your problems. It is not important that you may not have solved the problem; what is important is the way in which you have handled, or are handling it.

Many things are given to you as you go through life, some good, some which you would not rather have at all. Even when pleasant experiences or good things come into your life, there is something to be learned from them. Do you remember to be thankful for the good? Have you learned to share happiness or abundance with others? There is a lesson in everything that comes your way. Have you learned your lessons today? Or, do you just take what comes your way with no further thought, using or abusing the good that has come to you and never once pausing to give thanks?

When an unpleasant experience or some "bad luck" comes into your life, the cry goes up, "Why me, Lord?", or "Oh, God, help me." Very rarely do we hear anyone shouting, "Thank you, Lord!" when someone receives their share of God's blessings. Not many stop to ask, "Why me, Lord?" or say "I don't deserve this, Lord, but I thank you." Yes, there are lessons to be learned. Learn to be grateful, to give thanks freely to God. Look around you each day at the small miracles and the wonders in your life and be thankful. Praise God, for without Him you are nothing, and you have nothing.

When you are happy, learn to share your happiness with others, even those you do not know. Happiness inside should reflect happiness outside, and your smile should light the lives of those you meet along your way. Sharing; so few of you share the goodness and the blessings given to you each day. You take them for granted and keep them to yourself. Learn your lesson. Be giving of yourself and also be generous with your possessions and share, whenever you can.

I realize that it is difficult to understand why you have hardship and grief thrust upon you. I also realize that it is easy for someone to tell you to look for the good in every bad situation, especially when they don't seem to have any problems at all, but you must learn to do this. Something good does come out of everything that happens in your life. Instead of lamenting, "Why me, Lord?", ask yourself "What am I supposed to be learning from this situation?", and then set your mind to either finding a way to solve the problem, or to learning how to understand it and to accept it. You may never see any tangible proof that there was something good derived from that particular situation, but if you have learned your lesson, you will see that there are many intangible benefits. Are you not stronger, or perhaps more understanding? Have you not learned to be more gentle with those around you? If you really look, you will see what good has come to you because of some adverse condition in your life.

Most of you hang on to the memory of a bad situation, and you bring it up every chance you get, even though no one really wants to hear about it again. Why do you hold on to it so tightly? If you can't figure out what it was you were supposed to have learned from the situation, bless the situation and let the memory of it go. If you let go, perhaps, in time, you will be able to understand why this was given to you, and, if there is nothing else to be learned from it, at least you will have learned to let go of the past.

Yes, I know that you cannot stop to examine every minute of your life trying to figure out what your lesson is to be; however, you can go through life doing the best you can with every situation that comes your way, whether it be good or bad. There are some who do not know how to handle good properly, just as there are those who cannot handle adversity. God only expects you to do your best in everything and, in this way, you will learn much, even though you do not understand the lessons clearly when they are given.

You must never forget that life is one big classroom and, as you go through each step of your life, it is like going through a book, chapter by chapter. It is not enough to flip through the pages and then wonder why you haven't become any more understanding or any more knowledgeable. You must study as you go through life—and learn—for every situation, every condition, is given to you for a reason. Somewhere, therein, lies a lesson to be learned by you.

We here in spirit try so hard to help you to understand the value of these lessons, and, we also try to help you understand what the lesson is. It is very disheartening for us, however, when we find that most of you are not aware of the help we try to give you. You are so busy with your problems and worrying about self, that you do not stop to listen to us. When God created man and placed him on Earth, He gave man the ability to communicate with those in the unseen world. If there were problems that could not be solved, or questions that could not be answered, man had only to attune himself to the higher vibrations, and he would be in touch with those on the other side of life, who were willing to help him. And, not only willing, but, in fact, *waiting* to come to his aid. I have mentioned previously in this book that we, here on the other side of life, are assigned tasks which we are to complete in order that we may progress to the next level of our spiritual development. If we are assigned to help those on Earth, and we are never given the opportunity to do so, we must wait and wait, and our progression is very slow. For, we can try as hard as we like to get through with our messages and our suggestions, but if man is not aware that there is help from an unseen source, there is nothing we can do.

It is true, that in the past few years there has been a new awakening. Many of you are into meditation, Yoga, and other forms of mind discipline. This is good. As time goes on, you will see much more spiritual growth in man, as a whole. We are pleased with this growth, for it brings together our plane of existence and yours. Most people do not know, or do not wish to acknowledge, that their "inner voice" is really an outer voice, which comes from another plane, but that is exactly what it is. How is your "intuition"? Pretty good, you say? Where do you think these intuitive feelings come from? From God? From your "inner voice"? Certainly, for all things come from God, but it is through us that He communicates with you and gives you these intuitive feelings.

Have you had any interesting dreams lately? You say that some of them have been more than just dreams; that they have been precognitive and the events actually happened? How do you think you get this information? It is programmed here, on the other side of life, and we send it along to you, just as a television program is sent to you after it has been prepared.

If you would acknowledge the source of your intuitive feelings, and then begin to ask us for help with your problems, for answers to unanswerable questions, you would then become aware that there is, indeed, much more to life than what you see with your physical eyes.

Chapter **IV**
THERE IS A BEACON

I have tried to give you some idea, in the previous chapters, of how to develop your spiritual growth while you are still in the physical body. Remember, the more highly evolved you are spiritually, the more rewarding your experience, when you cross over to this side of life. I will repeat one thing, and then we will go on. Always try to be *the best you can be,* in everything you do. When you give of yourself, give the *best* of yourself, for this shows that you are really trying, and it is in the trying that you grow.

While it is true that there is no "Hell" as most of you picture it, with fires blazing eternally and no chance for one's spirit to escape, there are circumstances here which are not pleasant, and it is up to you to decide how pleasant, or unpleasant, your life will be when you cross over to this side of life.

There are many here who are troubled and lost. Those who do not prepare themselves spiritually while on Earth, do not enter here through The Garden, as I did, but must come by many other pathways, some of which are very dark. No one, however low he may be in the ladder of spiritual evolvement, no one is ever shut off completely from the "Light". What does happen, is that those who are not aware that life is continuous or that there is the chance for development and growth over here are so confused and frightened when they make the crossing that they are not aware of the Light shining in the distance. They go around in circles wondering what is to become of them and what they are to do.

No one is ever alone when they make the crossing, but, here again, most of those who are not spiritually evolved to some extent, are not aware that we are beside them, even on the darkest path, and that we try to make them aware of the Light and aware of us. They do not hear and they do not see. That is another reason why it is so important that you become aware of us while you are still on Earth. When you make the transition, you will know that there is someone beside you, guiding you along the way. Someone to tell you how you can progress so that you may leave the dark pathway and step out into the Light and enter through The Garden.

How long you who are unaware will have to stumble and grope your way along the dark pathway is up to you. As soon as you are able to hear us and to understand that there is room for growth here, you will begin to move out of the darkness. Once you have become aware of your lessons here and begin to go about the business of learning and of developing yourself to a higher degree of spirituality, you can then move along at your own pace. If you have not lived your life on Earth in the manner in which you should have lived it, there will be many lessons for you to learn here. However, one of the nice things about this side of life is that there is no time, as you know it there. What would seem an eternity to you is nothing to us. So you see, though you may have many lessons to learn here and much to do in order to get off the dark pathway, there is always hope. If you are sincere in your efforts, you can progress very rapidly and be ready to walk in the Light.

There are many here who make no progress at all. They cannot or will not see that there is something better for them just up ahead. We try to tell them, but they do not hear. You who are still on Earth can sometimes be of great help to these wandering souls, for, where they are not aware of us, they can hear you, and you can reach them many times when we cannot. If you know of someone who has left their physical body before they have made the effort to grow spiritually, you can help them if you will but think of them, and in your thoughts tell them to "look for the Light". For, once they have become aware of the pinpoint of Light at the end of their dark pathway, they are going in the right direction, and it is usually much easier for us to get them to listen after they have turned in the right direction. They, in heading toward the Light, become less confused and are more receptive to our thoughts. Yes, to our "thoughts". We, here on the other side of life, do not communicate as you do there, with your voice. We send thoughts which are picked up by others here just as you pick up the spoken word.

Once these confused spirits become aware of our thoughts, they can then more readily be aware of our presence, and when that happens, we can begin to work with them for they are no longer as frightened as they were when they thought they were alone in the darkness. They are on their way home.

Very few of you there on Earth expect to "die" before you have reached a ripe old age. Perhaps you say at some time or other, "When I die", or "if anything happens to me", but you never really expect anything to happen until you get much older. This is not a bad thing, as you would not enjoy life if you thought that every moment was your last. However, you should be prepared for the time when you do pass on, no matter when that time comes to you. Be aware that there is life unending, and prepare yourself so that no matter when your time comes to depart from that plane, you will not be frightened and you will understand that you are never alone. Tell yourself that should you pass on because of some traumatic experience, an accident, or an illness, that you will find peace the moment that your body is no longer alive. Know that there is no need to become bewildered and lost, no matter how traumatic your "death" may be. Once you have escaped the physical body there is no trauma, no pain, only peace, if you are ready to accept it. Be prepared. Some live long on Earth, some do not. Know what to expect when you leave there and you will never become lost on the other side.

We, here on this plane of existence, are saddened when we see the unprepared floundering and groping in the dark. There is no need for this. You must begin to open your minds and your hearts to the fact that there is more to life than what you see with the physical eyes and that the continuance of life is a beautiful thing, even though you are no longer encased in a physical body. Perhaps I should say,—*because* you are no longer encased in a physical body.

Many of you plan for a journey that you may never take, perhaps to Hawaii, or to Europe, or to the Orient. Still, it is good to think about it occasionally, even though you are not certain that you will be able to go. Why not, then, plan for the journey which you know you will be taking one day? The journey to your home. It doesn't take much effort to do this. All you have to do is to be aware that there is a continuance of life; that once you have departed from the physical body there is nothing to fear. Know that if you search out the Light, you will be on your way. While you are on Earth, God has made all sorts of provisions for you to receive help. You are never really alone. And, thus it is when you make the transition. Be prepared, and you will be aware as you cross over, that there are others there waiting to assist you at all times. Do not be frightened, for there is nothing to fear. We are here.

Chapter V
"AND BEAUTY SURROUNDS YOU"

I will try, as we go on now, to make you aware of some of the beauty that surrounds me here on the other side of life. It is difficult to put things into words, for the colors, the music, the flowers and trees here are so different from anything that you have experienced that it is difficult to try to make you see them as we do.

I talked to you of The Garden through which I had entered when I made my transition, some time ago. There is such a profusion of greenery that it is breathtaking and yet, one does not feel that he is being engulfed by this as one would in a jungle, but rather, that he is surrounded by peace and harmony. The breeze is gentle as it stirs the leaves of the trees and shrubs, and you almost feel that someone has caressed your cheek at it passes. There is music. One cannot tell exactly what the source is for it, as it seems to be everywhere and, still, it is so lovely that it seems to be part of The Garden itself.

Flowers, everywhere. If I were an artist, I would still have difficulty telling you about them, describing their shapes and colors, for they are like nothing you have ever seen, and the colors are exquisite. Some of the flowers are old favorites, but even they have taken on a new life here. Have you ever seen a rose so vibrantly alive that it can almost speak to you? Sometimes I am not sure that it did not speak to me as I gazed at it. For, there in The Garden, I had the feeling of voices all about me, and, yet, it was not an intrusion, for everything blends harmoniously together.

For a moment, picture in your mind the most colorful and beautiful bird that you have ever seen, and hear the song of the most beautiful songbird you have ever heard. These are mere shadows of what you will see and hear in The Garden. Butterflies and birds dance through the air, and there is a feeling of joy and happiness as you watch them, for they are so graceful and so beautiful that you know that they, too, must feel the peace and contentment that you feel here.

You have streams and lakes there on Earth, but you cannot imagine the beauty of the stream which flows through The Garden. The water is so crystal-clear that, were it not for the reflections seen upon it, and for the diamonds of light dancing on its surface, you would think there was nothing there at all. And, even the water seems to whisper to you as it bubbles and turns along its way. The greatest composers there on Earth could not take these sounds and put them together in the way that God has done here. The beauty one sees here and the sounds one hears all blend together so harmoniously that one is not quite sure where sound ends and sight begins.

As it is with all who enter through The Garden, I would have been content to remain there forever, but, once you have rested a while and become comfortable with the idea that you are no longer a part of the physical world, someone will come along to guide you along the pathway which leads to The University, which I have mentioned previously. As you go along the way from The Garden to The University, there are rolling green fields, and beauty all around. You see groups of children playing along the way, perhaps, or "people" walking along, or resting under the trees. I say "people" for even though we do not have physical bodies, as you do, we can take on the appearance of our former body and, thus, retain our individuality. You will not, however, see anyone here who is crippled or lame, or disfigured in any way. For, once the physical body is left behind, so are the problems which caused the manifestation of these conditions. Everything and everyone here is beauty, and harmony.

As one approaches The University, there are winding pathways lined with flowers. The building is white, but how can I describe the whiteness of it? It is like new snow when the sunlight sparkles on it, early in the morning. And, yet, that is not quite right. However, it is as close as I can come to giving you a description. For, you have to behold it to understand. There is always much activity here at The University, for new arrivals are constantly being brought there, to receive their assignments. Also, there are classrooms in The University for those of us who are ready to progress and to learn more about God, about life, and of our part in God's great plan. If you have ever gone to college, you know what the campus is like at the peak hours, and so it is here, with students coming and going. There are also classrooms here for the study of music or art, drama or any one of a thousand things to add to the beauty of one's life here.

If you have knowledge of some subject which others may wish to learn, you may become an instructor at The University, for, whatever you have to offer, no matter how inconsequential it may seem to you, is welcomed by someone else. And so, it is a giving and a taking here, as it should be there on Earth. Each one gives what they have to give, and each receives in return. This is what makes for peace and harmony in our lives here.

There are rooms here, also, where one may go to consult those who are more advanced in regard to any problems that may arise concerning one's assigned tasks. You must understand that when we cross over to this plane of life, we do not become all-knowing and versed in every subject. We have our problems, just as you have there. You, there on Earth, are usually reluctant to admit that you cannot handle a difficult task and, therefore, many times you bungle it completely before you seek help. We, here, know that there are those who are wiser than we are when we first begin, and we are happy to have someone who will talk with us and help us with our problems.

You think, perhaps, that our tasks are easy here. This is not so, for most of them are related to helping others, not only here, in spirit, but there on Earth, also. It is very difficult to do one's work if those you are trying to help are not aware of you or if they refuse to listen when they do become aware. This is sad. We never *tell* anyone what they must do, but, rather, try to guide them as they go through life. They are always able to choose which way they will go, which path they will trod, and, always, we are ready to help if they would but seek us out and ask. But, I will talk more of this later. I was trying to give you some idea of what it is like at The University.

There are lecture halls, and meeting rooms and there are great halls where those who are working with music may come together and play in concert. These concert halls are immense, and yet, no matter where one is seated, each beautiful note, each delicate instrumentation may be heard without the slightest flaw. Each note, from each instrument, no matter how softly it is played, may be heard clearly and, still, there is a complete blending of all the instruments so that it sounds as though only one musician were playing. It is difficult to try to make you understand these things and to make you see and hear them as we do. If I were to tell you about "chocolate", or "ice cream" and you had never tasted or seen these things, you would have great difficulty in trying to imagine what they were like. So it is with my descriptions of life here on the other side. You can read about it, but you will never know fully the beauty and wonder of it until you have arrived here yourself. There are colors, and sounds and scents which you have never experienced. How can I, therefore, describe them to you so that you will understand? I can only try to do my best. Perhaps you will perceive enough of this beauty and joy that abounds here so that you will no longer fear the "unknown" and when it is time for you to make the transition, you will be prepared and, perhaps, even welcome it.

Do you know that children in spirit do not remain children forever? They progress and grow, even as they would had they remained on Earth. They do not even *wish* to remain as children forever, as they realize that there is much that they can learn and much they can do as they grow. When they have reached adulthood, they then remain as young adults. Even though they grow spiritually, they will never age, for no one grows "old" here on the other side of life.

One section of The University is solely for the children. There are no structured lessons for them to learn, and they are free to come and go as they please. They, as those of us who are older, are allowed to grow at their own rate of speed, and no one hurries them along. They are all eager to learn more of God and to understand more of life, but some are a little slower than others, and, that is as it should be.

Even the tiniest babies are accommodated at The University. One unit of the children's section is a nursery where babies are cared for and loved until they are ready to go out among the other children. It always seems as though we have more willing workers here than we do babies or children, for there are always those who are ready to care for the children and to teach them. There is so much love here that it would seem that it must spill out over the Earth and engulf everyone there. Unfortunately, most of you on Earth are not aware of the love that flows from us to you. If you were, the Earth would be as happy a place as our home.

Chapter **VI**
PROGRESSION

At your colleges and universities, there, on Earth, students study to reach one level of attainment and then another, and another, until they are awarded a degree in their chosen field. If they study for a very long period of time, and work very hard at it, they might receive a Master's Degree. As long as they can pass the required examinations and give the proper answers, they are "masters". How very different it is here.

We have Masters. And, we have many levels at which one may become a Master. Those of you on Earth who feel you know a little about this side of life believe that Masters here are only those spirits of the highest order. This is not so. There are Masters on every level of progression from the lowest rung of the spiritual ladder to the highest. For, if one learns the lessons as they are given and one grows to the point where he is then able to pass on his knowledge and understanding to others here, and on Earth, he is then given the honor of being called a Master. This is so, on every level of the spiritual development of those on this side of life. You must understand, however, that we, here, do not learn our lessons from a book. We learn by experiencing. Our lessons involve not only our own lives, but the lives of those we are to teach or to help in some way. We do not take a written test at the end of the assignment to see how we "score". We are tested every moment that we are involved in our assigned tasks. We are graded on everything we do in relation to these tasks. Some of us will become Masters, some will hardly progress at all. Here, even as there on Earth, there are those who fail to understand that there is always room for more growth and that growth is progress. I am sure you know of someone like that? They are probably the same now, spiritually and mentally, as they were 10 or 15 years ago, although the body is growing older. They just sit. They are content to be, rather than becoming. One should be growing and changing constantly. Each new day that is given to you is a chance to make a new beginning and to become a better, more spiritual you.

Don't be content to just be the way you are . . . be discontented. Not really discontent with everything, so that you are complaining your way through life, but have enough discontent in your soul to keep you searching and seeking new ideas and new ways to grow. Look for that little feeling inside you that tells you that "something is missing" even though you have everything you can have materially. That "little something" is your spirit, stirring up discontent in you so that you will begin to seek the spiritual path. Learn your lessons well, each day, and, when you think you have learned them, search out new ideas, new places, new people, new experiences which will help you to learn more and to grow again.

As we are graded here, while we work on our assigned lessons, you are also being graded as you work on yours there. The more highly spiritual you become and the more you progress while on the Earth plane, the better it is for you when you make the transition to the other side of life. You may find, that you have become a Master, on your level of spirituality, even before you have made the transition, so that when you reach the other side of life you will be given this honor.

In order for one who is a Master to progress to another level, he must be ready to take on new assignments, learn new lessons and, relinquish the title of Master until he has reached a point in the next stage of his development where he will be ready to receive this honor once again. Here is another reason why some do not wish to move along and to grow. They do not wish to give up the title, for it can make some feel very important. If they have not learned to put their own importance aside to go on to help others, they will stay at that particular level. Their titles will not be taken from them, for they have earned them at that level, but they will no longer be making progress spiritually, and until they decide that they must move on, there is nothing anyone else can do to help them.

Tests. One is always being tested. You are tested there and we are tested here. I think, perhaps, it is a bit easier for us, here, since we are not pressured by time, and there is so much love here. Someone is always ready to talk with us, or to listen to our problems. I feel, also, that we are more apt to seek help and guidance when we have reached an impasse, while most of you on Earth are unaware that there is help and guidance available to you, at any time. We are always ready to help and guide you but cannot do so if you are unaware of what we tell you.

There was a time, long ago, when man understood and listened to the voice which guided him and advised him as he went through life, but the ability to do this has diminished over the span of time, and there are few now who understand, or are willing to understand, that this is possible still. When God created Earth and placed man there, He did not leave you alone, nor was your spirit to be separated from the world it had known. God left man with the ability and the understanding to communicate with the other side of life so that there would always be a tie between man and spirit. It saddens me to think that such a wonderful gift could be so soon forgotten. For, as man developed and became wiser in earthly matters, he became less and less aware of the spiritual side of his life and no longer used the gift of communication which God had given him. And, even now, man in the midst of his troubles wonders why God has deserted him when, in truth, God is there if man would only listen and be aware of his presence. For, it is through spirit that God communicates with man, and it is through spirit that God does his work. Therefore, it is pleasing to God and to us when we find those who are aware and are willing to communicate with us for it is then that we can do our work and progress spiritually.

You should see what it is like here when a new medium, a new channel, opens up for us to use to communicate with others who are not aware. It is like opening day at the ball park, with everyone here trying to be the first through the gate. Fortunately, we do have rules here and there are those who are placed in charge to see that everyone does not get through. If a person is at all spiritually evolved, there is no reason to be afraid of spirit communication, for there is always someone standing at the door to keep out those who would be unwelcome. If, however, someone of you there, on Earth, decided that he would like to try spirit communication just to see what he can do, and, if he uses this as a game, he could be heading for trouble. If one is seeking nothing more than thrills and excitement, this is exactly what one will get, but it may not always be pleasant excitement.

If one is sincere and wishes to use spirit communication to help oneself, or to help others, then we are here to see that no harm comes to that person and that unwanted entities do not interfere. It does not matter at what stage of spiritual development you are, if you are sincere in your work with spirit, there is nothing to fear. Rather, you will find that you have opened up a whole new world for yourself for you are attuned to life's higher planes.

Things are changing there on Earth, and more and more people are opening themselves up and "listening". Most, however, do not acknowledge that they are dealing with spirit when they "hear a voice", or "get a feeling" which tells them something. They say it is their intuition, or an inner voice which gives the information. Certainly, but your inner voice and your intuition is merely your spirit becoming attuned to us and transmitting the information to you. It matters not where you believe the information comes from as long as you can get the message. However, those of you who do acknowledge that it comes from spirit and willingly work with us, will find that you receive the messages more easily, for we are pleased that you are aware of our presence, and we try that much harder to help you. The more you communicate with us, the more you will understand how we work and the more we can be of benefit to you.

We can teach you anything you wish to know and tell you of things you have never heard before. We can teach you music, art, language and much, much more. We have the finest teachers in the Universe waiting to help you.

Do not be afraid to call on us whenever you wish. We are happy to be at your service, as long as you are honest and sincerely wish to work with us for the accomplishment of good.

Chapter VII
"LET THERE BE LIGHT"

Do you ever wonder what happens to those who are not prepared, spiritually, for the journey to the other side of life? What of those who have lived a life far removed from God, who have killed and robbed and done everything possible to hurt others? Where do they go?

As you have probably guessed, they come here in a state of utter confusion. They have no idea where they are, or what is expected of them. They weep and they moan as they flounder around in the darkness. Some who have never thought about God before now cry out for God to help them. What a pity that they have waited so long to seek Him. God is there, but He does not reach out His hand and take them from this place of darkness, for they must find the way; each at his own pace and at his own level of understanding. Those who are willing to listen, as we show them how to begin to make amends for the wrong they have been doing, will progress more quickly than those who are unwilling to listen. Many refuse to believe that there is a way for them to move out of the darkness and to become a more spiritual being. There is nothing we can do to help them until they understand. Usually when one or two begin to progress and move out of the darkness, others, then, become aware that there is a chance for them, also. But there are always those who doubt and must remain where they are until they, too, are ready to begin their progress.

Those who have come to The Place of Darkness must now rebuild their lives, and they must go back to the time when they began to live in a manner that was not pleasing to God. They must look at themselves and really see what they had been before coming here. This is not an easy thing to do. While on Earth, they were involved in things, rather than

31

just watching things happen, and, thus, they were not aware of the feelings of others, nor of the consequences of their own actions. Now, watching these scenes as they are recreated, they can feel what others felt and they can see the results of what they have done. Most cannot believe, though they have seen these things with their own eyes, what havoc they have caused.

When the past has been reviewed and discussed, it is time for the entity to begin his work. It is necessary for him, now, to try to help those whose lives have been disrupted because of his actions. For, nothing that is done on Earth can be done without affecting someone, somewhere. You have probably heard, many times, "but, I didn't hurt anyone". Nothing could be further from the truth. Every action touches someone.

Perhaps to you it seems that this would not be too difficult a task, helping others should be fairly easy.—Have you ever tried to help someone who just turned a deaf ear to you, or has someone hung up the phone in your ear when you tried to give advice? Imagine, then, how frustrating it is to those here when they are trying to be helpful to someone who is not even aware that they exist. Spirit must try and try, until such time when that person does, through intuition, or through a dream, or, perhaps, through a medium, heed the advice and accept the help offered. Occasionally, we do step in. When we see that spirit has really tried and there seems to be no hope of success, we show that it might be easier to send help to this particular person through another human being, perhaps a friend, who might be more receptive.

Each time a task is completed, the troubled spirit becomes a little more understanding, a little more loving, and, thus, begins to become a more spiritual being. It is very rewarding to us to watch these changes in one who had never thought of goodness, kindness, or love. We can actually see them grow. Where there had been a tight little, huddled mass of a being, there begins to be expansion and a reaching out to touch others. As they grow more and more spiritual, through their efforts to help others, the tiny spark of life within begins to grow and to glow, until they have completed these tasks and the warmth of their love radiates from them.

Now, they begin to understand the error of their ways when they were on the Earth plane. They understand the meaning of the words, "It is never too late." If they had heeded these words when they had been living in the flesh, they would not have had to go through this period of darkness and growth here. At any time, anywhere along the way, they could have begun to change, to become a more spiritually evolved being. If, while on the Earth plane, they had taken the opportunity, for even one minute, to try to be a better person, to help, rather than hurt others, a tiny spark would have been lit over here, to start them on their way. Each time there is another change in the human heart, the spark along the pathway, here on this plane, grows brighter and leaps to light another. Should the person continue to grow spiritually, on earth, by changing his ways, the sparks continue to burn and leap, until the pathway is lit with many sparks and when the spirit crosses over there is illumination and he then begins to find his way.

Yes, he must make amends for the wrongs that he has done previous to his change of heart, but think how much better it is to come in to a new town or a new home that has been lighted for you, rather than into complete darkness. Even though you are unfamiliar with the new surroundings, there is comfort in the light which surrounds you.

Growth and change come much more easily to those of you who are on the Earth plane. It is so much easier for you to become a more spiritual individual before you make the crossing over to the other side of life. I'm sure you can understand this. There are so many opportunities for you to do good and to be kind and loving to those with whom you come in contact, that you can grow very rapidly. Even though you may have hurt someone along the way, it is much easier to make amends while you are still in the body. Once you reach the side of life where you are spirit, you will find that it is much more difficult to reach those you have left behind. For, most people believe that once you have passed on, you are no longer able to communicate with them, nor they with you. And, so, try as you may to help them, you will find it extremely difficult to get through to them.

There are many who believe, and rightly so, that each day is the first day of their lives. For, each day is a new beginning. But, remember this! Each moment of your life is also a new beginning, and you have the opportunity to change or to "begin anew", at any time. Don't wait. Seize each opportunity for growth, for advancement, for the chance to become the new you. Begin now, to light your pathway. No matter what your life has been in the past, "It is never too late" to begin again, at any moment. But, do not wait until there are no moments left. For, when your life on Earth is done and you make the transition to the other side of life, you will find it more difficult to change your ways.

Chapter VIII
THE CHILDREN

Sooner or later, in everyone's life there comes a time of parting, when one you have known leaves the Earth plane. I am sure you have all wondered what was in store for the person who had "died", as you would call it. As I have explained to you previously, there are many avenues open to one who passes on, to the other side of life. I will discuss some of these avenues with you. In this chapter, we will begin with the children.

When a child is chosen by God to return to Him, there is joy here. As you rejoice there at the time of a new birth, so do we rejoice here, for it is the homecoming time. We know that there will be sadness and loneliness there for you, but we have also known sadness when the child left us to be born in the human form. Now the child comes home, to us.

There is a pathway into The Garden which is reserved for children. No adult may come this way. Angels stand watch at the entrance gate and turn away adults who may have accompanied a child to the gate, or some adult who may have become confused and found himself at the wrong entrance. Those who are turned away at the Children's Gateway, are always given direction and instructions on how to reach their rightful entrance.

Children are so pure in heart that they have a special place here and everything possible is done to make them feel at home. Some children are a little apprehensive when they first arrive, but they all learn to adjust very quickly, as children do, to their new surroundings.

Upon entering The Garden gate, the newcomers are met by groups of children from this plane. They are taken by the hand and led down the pathway, through The Garden, always being allowed to stop and rest, if they desire to do so.

Or, perhaps they wish to wander about a bit and look at the birds and the tiny animals which scamper about. The animals and birds have no fear and come close so that they may be touched and loved. For, even as children's hearts are pure, so are the hearts of these creatures. Occasionally, the children will stop along the edge of the beautiful stream which flows through The Garden to watch the fish as they sparkle beneath the water's surface, catching the rays of sunlight like the facets of a jewel. The children take great delight in putting their feet into the water and though the water is cool to the touch and refreshing to drink, it is never so cold that one is shocked by it as you might be in one of your mountain streams. Refreshing; everything about The Garden is refreshing, from the color of the sky to the velvet-like softness of the grass. The colors of the flowers blend and intermingle with each other so that sometimes you are not quite certain where one begins and another ends.

No child is ever hurried along, for they may take all the time they wish to reach The University, where they will be turned over to the care of those who will be in charge of their training. There is no need to rush here. For, time is unimportant, and the main thing is to see that the children are comfortable and relaxed in their new surroundings. We would never wish to frighten them or to make them unhappy here.

As each child completes his or her walk through The Garden, they are brought to The University where they go to the office of the registrar. The name of the child will be placed in the record book of those who have entered, and the registrar will then examine the child's records and see where the child is to be placed. We are very careful about placement. For these children to grow and progress as they should, they must be placed in the care of those who understand the particular lesson each child must learn; one who has experienced the same lesson at some time, either while on Earth, or over here.

Once the child becomes accustomed to being out of the physical body, to the new surroundings, and to his new "family", he is then ready to begin his new life.

Contrary to what you might think, the children do not play all day and romp through the meadows with no thought of anything else. They have studies, the same as they would if they were still in the physical body, there on Earth. However, there is a relaxed atmosphere here which makes learning such a joy that one does not "have to" learn a lesson, one "wants to".

Babies, of course, do not have lessons to learn. They are cuddled and loved as you would love them. Perhaps I should not have said that they do not have lessons to learn, for they are learning all of the time, as they grow. What I should have said was that they do not have specific lessons outlined for them, as the older children do. The babies grow at their own rate of speed, just as any normal, healthy child would do on Earth.

Toddlers are taught, along with the necessary basic skills, music: not so much how to play music, but how to "feel" it. They are taught to listen, to absorb, to move with the music, to become a part of it. Music is one of the most beautiful gifts that God has given us, and the children are taught to enjoy it with every part of their being. These little ones are also taught about art. Not to draw, or to paint, but to "feel" the beauty of color, and shape and form; to become a part of the tree, the flower, or the bird which they see. As they grow older, they may never have the desire to play a musical instrument, or to paint a picture, but they will have learned to experience the true beauty of music and all of the other wonderful things which God has created. You have heard, perhaps, someone speak of "Heavenly Choirs", or "Celestial Music" but until you, yourself, experience this music, you cannot know how truly beautiful it is. For, we not only sing or play the music, we *become* the music and there is nothing on earth that can equal the sound. That is why we take such care in teaching our children.

As the babies and toddlers grow and progress, they move from the nursery to other classrooms in The University and other areas of life here. Again, they are placed with those who will help them on their way. When the child is at an age where he or she has definite ideas about what their interests are, we try to schedule classes for them where these interests will be met. I say "try", for there are some children who would want to do everything at once, and we must determine what is best for them at a particular time. We do not want them to have no time for leisure, for frolicking about with their friends or just enjoying the beauty that is all around.

It is a pity that the classrooms of your schools on Earth do not reflect the atmosphere of our classrooms here. There is a feeling of warmth, relaxation and peace as one enters the classroom, and, always, the feeling of genuine love. Here, it is a joy to study and grow, not a task. Teachers are looked up to for each of us realizes that the teacher would not be in this position if he were not prepared to do the work as it should be done, with understanding and love.

Sounds Heavenly, doesn't it? A school with no problems in the classroom. But, that is exactly what we have here, a Heavenly University. Remember, in this chapter I have been telling you of the children, and relating to you the various stages of progression which they go through. Because they are young, they do not have many lessons to unlearn from their lifetime on Earth, and they quickly progress to The University. Infants, toddlers, and the majority of children, even through their teen years, have few lessons carried over when they make the transition.

There are, of course, exceptions to everything.

All of the children who have departed from their physical bodies and moved on to the other side of life do not enter this plane of existence through The Garden. As I mentioned previously, there are many avenues by which one may enter. Let us take, for example, the child who had never, in his lifetime, done anything that was expected of him. Every rule was broken. Rudeness, disobedience, obstinence were such a part of this child that one would call him "a little monster". What becomes of such a child when he leaves the Earth plane? Surely, even though God loves children dearly, He cannot possibly treat this one as he would one who was obedient and kind.

God does have other plans for one such as this. For even though God does love him, he must learn to become more God-like himself, before he can be allowed to enter The Garden and then go on to The University. This may take some time, depending upon the child himself. You, perhaps, know how difficult it is to get through to a child who is obstinate, one who blocks his ears, heart and mind to anything and everything you may say or do. We, here, have the same problems. It is extremely difficult for us to reach such a child, and that is why it takes so long for them to begin to make any progress at all. They are never deserted, even though we would like to say "forget it" and leave them to themselves. We try everything we can to make them aware of the fact that they are not lost and that they can move on to a place far more beautiful than they have ever seen or imagined. We tell them that there are others waiting to greet them and many exciting new things for them to do and see, but they turn a deaf ear to us. Thank God that we who are in charge of these children have already learned the lessons of patience and understanding for, otherwise, we could not work so diligently at our appointed task. Occasionally, one or two will be more willing to listen and they then become more interested in us and what we have to offer, than they are in themselves.

Quietly, we stand and wait, and when we feel it is time, we try once more to awaken something in these youngsters that will let them move on, out of the dark corner where they must stand until they forget about trying to win and try, instead, to find something better for themselves. It is difficult work, for it makes us sad when they do not want to listen, and they do not believe.

Once a child understands that we are there to help them, they begin to listen, and that is the first lesson they will have learned,—to listen. From that point on, the going, for us, is much easier. At last, we are getting through! We, then, have to teach this child about obedience, how to obey the rules and why rules and laws are important in one's life. When the child begins to understand these teachings, we then go on to kindness, to manners and whatever else has been lacking.

Perhaps you feel that this child will be in the corner of darkness forever, with all of these lessons to be learned. It would seem so, but this is not necessary. When the child has an *understanding* of what is expected of him and what he must do to become a better individual, he is allowed to move out of the corner of darkness and move to other areas of life here, where he can be more comfortable. Here the child can feel less bewildered and less defensive, for he can see that there are others who are learning the same lessons that he has to learn.

Here, as on Earth, children tend to follow-the-leader. If, in a group of newcomers to the corner of darkness, there is not one who will let down the barriers and respond to us, no one will want to be first. But, just let one of them waiver, and they all become willing listeners, for no one wants to be left behind. Children are children, wherever they are.

From the corner of darkness, the children who have learned to understand what is expected of them, and what they can expect in return, are moved to other areas. Some will be guided along the pathway through The Garden, but others will be guided to areas which are brighter than where they were previously, but still outside The Garden wall. We work very closely now with these children and, for the most part, it is not long before they, too, are led through The Garden.

All children are not sweet and gentle, as one would picture them. But, on the whole they are not too bad. One can over-look their faults and try to understand that because they are children, they have much to learn. With love and patience most of them grow to be fairly decent adults, who have something good to contribute to the society in which they live. Again, however, there are exceptions.

What becomes of the children who are so twisted up within themselves that they can commit acts which would be horrifying to us even if an adult committed them? Robbery, torture of animals or of other children, murder. What happens to these poor souls when such children pass on?

You would expect them to be dealt with very harshly once they arrive here on the other side of life, would you not? They have done terrible things, and they must be punished severely! . . .

No, they are not punished any more than the other children who come to us. For a child to commit any one of the acts which we have mentioned, his mind and heart would have to be very confused. And, if the mind and heart were confused, would not the soul be in the same condition? To make matters worse, the state of confusion they experienced on Earth was nothing compared to the state of confusion they are in once they leave the physical body behind. They flounder around in the darkness and cry for help and they feel, as they did on Earth, that there is no one, to help or to hear their cry. Because they wander about in the darkness, it is more difficult to reach them. They are aware of nothing but the darkness and their own helplessness.

We, here in spirit, try to be even more gentle and understanding with these poor souls. We must reach out to them and gently, lovingly, quietly, try to bring them to a state of less confusion, where they can become aware that there is help available to them if they will only accept it. They will, of course, have many, many lessons to learn once they begin to be more receptive, and it will take so much longer for them to progress and grow. While they committed whatever terrible act they had, while on Earth, the full impact of it did not reach them because of the state of mind they were in at the time. As they learn the lesson of understanding here, the full realization of what has been done will come to them. This, then is their punishment, for they must live with this realization, here, until they can learn the lesson of forgiveness and truly forgive themselves. This is a most difficult task, for it is much easier to forgive another than to forgive oneself.

Chapter **IX**
PURGATORY, HEAVEN AND HELL

Mankind has always wondered what lies beyond the grave. One hears so much about the "Heaven" which awaits on the other side of the veil which separates your plane of existence from ours. In dying does man immediately ascend to some paradise? Or, as some believe, does man then go to a place called "Purgatory", where one must remain until his sins are forgiven? And, what of "Hell"? Why do you worry so much about what is waiting for you when you die? What you should be worrying about is what you are doing with your daily lives. For, therein, lies the key to what you will experience when you depart from this life which you now know.

If your life on Earth is such that you wallow in mud, can you expect something better when you pass on? Some feel that no matter how they live now, once they leave the physical body, they are "all set" and they are immediately taken to a place of paradise, Heaven. How foolish! This is like expecting one who has been a traitor to his country to be buried with full military honors. True, there is no place here on the other side of life where one is engulfed in flames to cleanse the soul, but your life on Earth will determine how quickly you will progress once you move on, and how long you will remain in darkness there. If one cannot understand what is right and what is good while on Earth, how long will it take for one to understand what it is we are teaching over here? If a person has lived a life of doing wrong and associating with those of like character, how will that person be able to relate to us? Are we to be trusted when we tell of better things awaiting just over the hill? Progression is very slow, indeed, for such as these. They can, and some do, remain in the darkness for what would seem to be an eternity. They have not been banished, nor are they being persecuted for their unholy lives. Their problems are of their own making. Until they can understand that we are here to help them along the way, to direct them and counsel them as they undo their previous mistakes, and learn the lessons which they must learn, we are unable to help them. We must, and do, from time to time, speak with them and try to get them to understand, but it is a very slow and difficult task. Some just never listen at all, and so they remain in that state of confusion and darkness, until such time as they are ready to learn, to understand, to listen. The flames which consume them are not the flames from fire, but the burning and anguish within themselves for they do not know where they are, or where they are going. Needlessly, they have created their own purgatory.

Purgatory and Hell are states of mind which the individual has created and with which that individual must live, until the awakening comes and one understands that it is not necessary to remain in that state forever.

Is there a "Heaven", a "Paradise"? Yes, there is. But, it may not be exactly as you have pictured it in your mind, nor is the gateway to Heaven locked to all but the few who have lived "saintly" lives.

You were not placed on Earth to sit atop a mountain, or in a cave to meditate all day and thus gain the key to Heaven. Nor, was it meant for you to become so aloof from your fellow human beings that nothing touches you and you are, therefore, almost perfect in every way. Life means involvement. How you live among others, is the important factor. This does not mean, however, that you "put up a good front" as the saying goes. If you are the type of person who puts on a good show when others are around so that you are always thought of as a "great guy", but when there is no audience, no applause, you revert to being anything but that, you will find when you get over here that your key does not fit the door, and you will have many lessons to learn before

44

you are ready to enter The Garden gate. You are not, as many would think, banished from Heaven forever. Your entrance is merely delayed, until you understand that you have made mistakes on Earth and that these mistakes have to be rectified.

The key that opens The Garden gate is UNDERSTANDING. It is not necessary that one correct all mistakes and undo all wrongs before one can be allowed to enter The Garden. It is only necessary that one begins to understand what was not right with the life they had lived while in the physical body and when the understanding of these things comes, the spirit is then able to easily open the gateway and move on. Understanding is the key to all things here. For, without understanding one cannot learn any of the lessons which are necessary for advancement and growth here.

That is why I have said that one does not need to be a "saint" while on Earth in order to attain Heaven. If an individual does not live as he should, but is aware of his shortcomings and transgressions while he is still in the physical body, and tries, as he goes through life, to correct these errors, to become a better individual, he is already forging the key to open The Garden gateway when he crosses over to the other side of life.

Again, it is the understanding of oneself which is important. For, if you understand your shortcomings, you are then able to make corrections as you go on through life. Being aware of your faults, however, and doing nothing about them will get you nowhere. Awareness is not understanding. You must be aware of the faults and then understand what is necessary for correction; what changes have to be made in your life. Then as you begin to make these changes, you are on your way.

Chapter **X**
LESSONS TO BE LEARNED

There are as many avenues beyond The Garden as there are those which lead to The Garden. However, once you have passed through The Garden, the going becomes much more pleasant. I speak of classrooms, and lessons which have to be learned, and, perhaps, you think of lessons such as music, or art, or drama. Yes, we do have these, but the more important lessons are the lessons which were left unlearned in one's lifetime on Earth. Love, kindness, sharing, humility, patience, and so many more that I could not begin to list them all. Most individuals have more than one lesson to learn when they come to The University and while we do have classrooms here for every lesson, the individual must also learn by "working in the field" so to speak. Therefore, each individual moves along the pathway on which will be found much opportunity to learn his particular lesson, by working with others in spirit and, also, by working with those who are still on the Earth plane.

An individual may choose to work on one lesson at a time, or more than one. It is his choice. Some find that by devoting more time to the one lesson that they accomplish much more than if they scatter their energies and try to do more than one. We all progress at our own rate here so there is never any pressure about finishing up the lesson and going on to another one. We each are given a list of the lessons to be learned when we first come to The University and we are given progress reports as we go along so that we always know how we are doing. It is not always easy to tell if one is making any progress, especially when dealing with those on the Earth plane, for we are not always aware that we are getting through to them. Those who are in charge, here, of marking our progress, however, can more easily check our progress by tuning in to the Earth plane to see if we have done our work well.

The counselors here are very helpful to us. When we feel that we have reached a point where we are not making any progress at all, they show us how to try a different approach, perhaps, or encourage us to try again. We are never made to feel that we are hopelessly floundering around without getting anywhere with our lessons. They are very kind and understanding, for they have all been through this and have learned their lesson well. Patience and understanding and love are there, as they counsel us.

These counselors are very wise and can answer most of our questions without any trouble. If, however, they find that there is something which we have to know and they are not familiar with the subject, or do not know the answer, they will call in someone else. There is no false pride here, or ego, and one does not stand in the way of another's growth by blindly leading him along, even though it may be in the wrong direction. We help here, we do not hinder, the soul's growth. The only one who can do that is the individual himself, for he can only grow spiritually at a rate which he, himself, will allow. Fast or slow, it is up to him. We do not prod or push. We do try to encourage those who are having problems, but if our encouragement is not well received, we stand back and wait until the time is right to again try to help that individual along the pathway.

Imagine that you are now here, in spirit, no longer attached to the physical body. You have been to The University, and you have been given your assignment. You would, just as you did there when undertaking a new assignment in your life, stand with your papers in your hand and say "What do I do now?" This is when a counselor steps in, to advise you and to start you on your way.

"May I help you?"

"Who,—me?"

Yes, you seem a bit bewildered."

"Oh, well . . . I have been told that I must study patience, and I don't seem to know where to begin to do this."

"Come, I will show you where to begin."

At that point, the counselor would take you to a quiet spot where you could sit and talk, and you would be on your way.

"Patience is your lesson. Now, you may begin by working with others in spirit, or you may do your work by reaching out to those on the Earth plane. Are there some there, perhaps, with whom you had no patience at all, or very little of it? Or, are there some back there who need also to learn the lesson that has been assigned to you?"

You feel that you would like to work with those to whom you showed a great deal of impatience, and, perhaps, help them while you are helping yourself to grow. The counselor teaches you how to tune in to the vibrations of those on Earth with whom you will be working. "Sounds easy, doesn't it?" It is not so simple and, therein, begins the lesson, for you must have the patience to keep trying until you can reach those with whom you are working.

Now, it is not always necessary for them to be aware that you are working with them, but you can tell when the lessons are being done correctly for, even though they are not aware that you have been talking to them, or trying to reach them, one day you will hear someone say, "Remember how impatient he was? I can understand now why he was that way, and I really do not blame him." Or, "Boy! you remember how impatient he was? Well, I've learned my lesson from that, and I will really try to be more patient with those who come into my life."

All of these things are noted by those who are in charge of your progress record. If you have been very patient yourself, in dealing with those on the Earth plane, this does not take as long as one would imagine. If you, however, are very impatient, again, the vibrations that are set up are such that you block the contact with those you are trying to reach, and you will have difficulty making any progress at all. If you begin to feel frustrated and feel that you cannot make any progress, talk with your counselor, and, perhaps, a change in your schedule will be made so that you can work with those in spirit rather than those on the Earth plane, until you become more accustomed to your new life. You may wish to continue as you were; if so, the counselor will advise you as to how you can make changes in what you are doing so that you are able to progress more quickly. There is always someone ready to help you. You are never alone here.

Most of you, who cross over, want to work with the Earth plane in the beginning, rather than with spirit, as it is more exciting to you to try to reach those you have left behind. Little do you realize that it is very difficult to do this unless you are dealing with someone who is very much aware that we do exist. It is much simpler for someone on the Earth plane to contact someone in spirit for we are always waiting and eager to work with you. Once someone on Earth becomes aware that they can communicate with us, the channel is always ready, whenever they wish to contact us. We, however, could try for an eternity to get through to one of you, and, if you were unaware that we exist, that life goes on, that there can be communication between our two planes, we would get nowhere. For, even though you felt our presence, or heard us, you would say it was your imagination, or a dream, or an hallucination. Thank God for those who are aware or do become aware that we are here. For it is through them that our work becomes much easier, and we are able to help those on Earth who need our help, whom we could not reach otherwise.

Be aware, understand that life does go on. Learn to work with us and to accept our help while you are still in the physical body, and then when you cross over to the other side of life, you will have no problem of adjustment, for it will be as though you have come back home to see your old friends, and that is as it should be.

Chapter **XI**
IT'S NOT TOO LATE

Now we continue along the paths of learning, here on the other side of life. Some of you have lessons to learn, in the arts. Perhaps you were given the gift of music when you were there on earth, but used it selfishly. Did you give freely of your music to those around you who would have enjoyed it? Or, did you play or sing when no one would hear, thinking that it wasn't important for you to share this gift with others, no matter how poorly you thought you would do if someone were listening. Were you given the gift of art work, in sketching, painting or creating things of beauty for others to see and enjoy? It does not matter that you were not a famous artist, for there are many ways in which you can give joy to others even when you are unknown. Keeping one's gifts to one's self is not what God had intended. They must be passed on to others in some way and enjoyed by all.

All right, so your voice wasn't that great. Did you ever try singing to a small child or to a baby, or, perhaps, to someone who was ill. What joy you would have given them. They care not that you do not have the voice of Caruso or some other famous singer. The gift you would have given would be a priceless treasure for it would lift their spirits for a moment, and would be remembered, and enjoyed over and over again.

You, who are on Earth, think that you can turn your back on these gifts and it is of importance to no one. This is not so. These gifts were given to be used, and to be used for the enjoyment of all. When you come over here, you must learn to make use of these gifts, and to give pleasure to others through them.

Perhaps you would classify these lessons as "sharing" or "working with others" and they are that too. But the main lesson is to teach you how to *use* your gifts to the fullest.

50

Can you recall conversations which you may have had while on Earth, which went something like this. A friend asks you: "Can you play the piano?"

"Well", you reply, "I play a little."

"Would you play for me?"

"Oh, I can't. I really don't play that well."

Who were you to judge what it was this particular friend was in need of at that time? Even if you had played a few notes, or some silly little ditty on the instrument, you might have struck an important chord inside that friend. Now, your lesson here is to give your gift to others. Everything sounds so simple. However, you will not find it that easy. You will be placed with a group, here in spirit, or back on the Earth plane, who are so caught up in themselves that they are not about to accept your music or anything else you have to offer them. (I have been speaking about music, but this applies to all areas; painting, sketching, dancing, drama.) Those with whom you will be working will be individuals who have never opened themselves up so that another individual could get close to them. They are self-centered, distrustful and only wish to be left alone. They must learn to accept kindness and gifts which are given freely to them. In working with them, you will find your task as difficult as they will find theirs. How much more simple it would have been if, while you and they were still on Earth, you had each done what was expected of you . . . giving to others and being able to accept that which was given.

For hours on end, you will sit at your instrument here waiting for someone to ask you to play for them. But, no one wants to hear your music. Then, you see someone back on Earth who would like to hear you play, for they had asked you many times. Ah! This is your chance. They will listen. And so you begin.

"What is happening? They are not listening! Hello, there! Can't you hear the music? You asked me to play for you. Why aren't you listening now?"

But, since they are not aware that you exist any longer, they proceed on their way, wondering, perhaps, why they had thought of you at that particular moment. And so it goes. One unsuccessful attempt after another. Will you ever be able to do what you should have done while you were still in the physical body? Are you to be forever trying and getting nowhere? No, eventually, you will find that someone will be receptive to your efforts, for, just as you wish to progress, there are others who will decide that they, also, wish to get out of their rut and to go on to something better. You will find, also, that there are some people on Earth who will be receptive to your efforts, as time goes on. As others begin to open up to you, you will make rapid progress, for then you will begin to understand what you had not done correctly and why these lessons are necessary now that you have crossed over to the other side of life.

This will give you some example of the difficulty of trying to undo the wrongs you have done on Earth, and trying to correct the omissions you have made while you were in the physical body. This applies to all areas of your life there, not only to the specific areas which I mention here, in this chapter of this book. Hopefully, when you have read this lesson which I have given you, you will understand and begin to change your way of life, if it needs change. It is never too late. You can begin at any moment to alter your life and to set up a better way of life for yourself when you cross over.

"Ah! I caught you!" There you sit thinking that these things do not apply to you. Your life hasn't been all that bad. You have tried to do the right thing, and when you get to the other side of life you will be all set to go on to advance work and not have to worry about anything from your life here.

"Think again." Each of you has some area of your life that can stand change, no matter how slight that change may be. It does not matter that you become perfect; it is only important that you *try* to change. For if you are trying, it means that you at least understand that there may be something better that you can do, or something better that you can be, in your lifetime on Earth. Understanding and trying. The key to spiritual growth.

Many of you have mottos hung in your office, or, perhaps, standing on your desk, or on the walls of your homes. "Think", "Do unto others", and so on. It would be far better if you would discard whatever it is you have there and put up a sign that says, "Begin Again". This would make all the others obsolete. To begin again means just that. Each moment of each day begin to make the adjustments and changes in your life that are necessary to your spiritual growth and necessary to your life as a human being. Remember, each thing that you do affects someone else, either directly or indirectly, even though you may not be aware of this. And, nothing that you do on Earth goes unnoticed here. The smallest effort to "begin again" is noted on your records here and when it is time for you to make the journey to the other side of life, all of the "new beginnings" will be to your advantage.

BEGIN AGAIN. Now.

Chapter XII
ELECTIVE STUDIES

"Are you growing weary of these lessons? Have I made you think, perhaps more than you would like to do?" We will digress a little from the lessons, and I will tell you more of the other departments of The University, where lessons of another sort are given. These, of course, would be more enjoyable.

When you have reached a point in your evolvement where you are ready for the finer things in life and for the extra-curricular activities which are offered at the University, you'll find there is nothing that an individual could possibly be interested in that is not taught here. And, by very competent teachers.

We have Masters in each department who have lived in ages past, and we have Masters who have advanced to such a degree that they have access to knowledge which is available nowhere else, for they reach into the future to obtain this knowledge. It is a pity that your schools on Earth do not have such teachers.

Do you wish to study Art? You may begin anywhere that you choose, taking just one type of art or going to the time when art was first used in its most primitive form and working your way through, to the present, or into the future. It is all here. Again, this does not apply only to this subject, which I have mentioned above, but to all things. Art, aviation, building, cooking, drafting, and so on, through all of the subjects from A to Z. You may pick and choose as you wish. One does not necessarily have to become an artist, etc., but may only wish to study the subject to gain more knowledge of that particular thing. You may wish to use this knowledge for your own advancement, or you may wish to teach others, as time goes on. It does not matter. There are classes geared to every individual's wants and needs, and if one should be lacking, it can be set up at a moment's notice so that the need may be fulfilled.

Studying is a pleasure here. Classes are very informal, and one moves along at one's own pace. There is never any pressure about not getting the lesson done, for you hold no one back but yourself, and how quickly you proceed is a personal matter over here. You may stay as long as you wish on one subject or on one lesson. There is plenty of time. Here, time is unimportant.

We have here famous architects, artists, musicians, magicians. The Great Houdini, who tried so desperately to make contact with the other side of life, when he was there on Earth, teaches here now. If you are familiar with his life story, you remember that he tried to contact his mother who had already passed on. It was unfortunate that he never realized that if he allowed himself to do so he could have contacted her personally, rather than running from one so-called medium to another. He tries to work with others on Earth who are having difficulty in understanding that it is possible to contact us. In doing this, he hopes to make it easier for someone to reach those in spirit and to know that life does continue once the physical body is left behind. Houdini also works with our students who are interested in learning the art of magic and illusion.

There are too many personalities here who teach in The University to mention them all by name. However, you will find as you talk with these Masters and Teachers, that they all knew, or felt, even as they lived on Earth, that they had been guided in their work by unseen forces. How else could they have written such outstanding books? Or composed such beautiful music? How then could physicians, who led the way for today's modern methods and medicines, have done all of the wonderful things which they accomplished, if it were not for Divine Guidance, given through spirit?

Everyone on Earth is not aware that he is divinely guided. If they write music or poetry, they may say that it is an inherited gift, something they must have gotten from one of their forefathers. Some, however, will understand and acknowledge that they are guided and aided by some unseen force, and when they reach this point, their work will far surpass what they would do had they not been aware of this.

Inventors. We have them here, also. Some with which you are familiar and some you have never heard of because they were so far before your time, or practically unknown, even in their own time. There are Masters here working on inventions which will be given at some time in the future, to someone on Earth who is receptive. It would amaze you to see the things that we see here. If it is important to us, we are allowed to look into the future and to take knowledge from that time and use it as is necessary. All of us are not allowed to look too far into the future and, to tell you the truth, we do not feel that is necessary, for, again, time is not important to us and we are happy and very busy with each moment that we experience here.

If it becomes necessary to secure information from the future to help someone, then we have access to this information, either directly, or through someone else, here in spirit, who will relay the information to us. In our classes, we may project into the future if there is something one wishes to know, in relation to his studies. Perhaps, an architectural student would like to see what is coming in the way of architecture centuries from now, in order that he may see the changes and trends. He has, perhaps, already studied this subject from the beginning of time and now wishes to see what other changes will take place. In a case like this, he is allowed to project into the future and to view these things for himself.

And, this is true in each classroom. In order to get a better overall picture of the subject being studied, a student may be allowed to project into the future. Students find that this is very helpful as it gives them a broader understanding of the entire subject.

Do you know that you may also do this? If you are aware of your spirit guides, and you work closely with them, they can, if it is necessary, show you or tell you many things that are important to your line of work, or your life. Are you doing something creative? Writing, composing, building, designing? If you need new ideas that haven't been tried yet, or seen by others, ask your guides, and they will help you to get glimpses of these things so that you may use them in your work. It is not difficult to do this; one must only be aware that we exist and that one can work with us. Once you are aware and open yourself up to us, we will go all out to aid you in whatever you do.

So many of you are hung up on the idea that everything you learn to do must come from books, or instructors. Not so. What did people do before there were books, or instructors? Someone invented musical instruments, and they played them before there was any written music to be read. Someone created stories and they were told before there were any written records, or books. How were all these wonderful modern conveniences which you use every day manifested? Someone had to have the idea and then build on that idea.

Do you wish to play an instrument? Perhaps you would like to write a book? Poetry? Whatever it is you desire to do, if the desire is sincere, can be done. What of all of those artists who just sit down and paint, never having had a lesson? What of musicians who cannot read music, and yet, their music surpasses any that was written? You would find, in talking with them, that they believe that there is something or someone which guides them in their work. They may not call it spirit, but may say, "Oh, I have help with my music", or "I just relax, and the music seems to flow through me. It's as though someone else were playing, at times". You, too, can do these things. I will tell you more of this a little later. Let us go back to what goes on at The University.

The classrooms in the University are spacious, airy and light. There is always a feeling of relaxation and peacefulness here. And, even though the atmosphere is really great, sometimes the lessons will be given outside the classroom, out on the grounds of The University. This is always a pleasure, and we look forward to taking our classwork outside. The grounds surrounding The University are very beautiful. There are winding paths and trees and flowers. Along the pathways one will find natural groves which make ideal settings for study areas. There are some benches here and there, which blend in so well with the natural setting, that they are almost a part of nature itself. Most of us prefer, however, when studying out of doors, to sit on the lush green grass and relax, as we feel the coolness of the earth beneath us. The singing of the birds is never distracting, as the music is a joy to hear, and we listen with pleasure as we work at our lessons. We never have to worry about sudden changes in the weather, such as rain, or cold, for it is always pleasantly warm here. Because of the beauty of the surroundings, one learns more quickly when studying out of doors.

Some of the students prefer to study in a more formal setting. If this is the case, they need only walk a little farther down the pathways and come to the formal gardens. Here, the gardens are laid out as you would, perhaps, see them on the grounds of a palace or some palatial estate. There are hedges and shrubs which are all neatly trimmed, and as you walk along you will see fountains and statues that are exquisitely beautiful. Some are fashioned from marble, and others are made of a stone which you have never seen or heard of and which is even more beautiful than marble for it is almost translucent. These have been made by sculptors who are Masters in the art, and it is impossible to describe their beauty to you. One day, you will see these statues for yourself, and you will understand.

In the formal gardens there are, also, benches placed about and, here and there, there are tables at which a few students may study together. Here, again, the surroundings are so peaceful and lovely that one has no difficulty in learning the lessons which have been assigned.

We have outdoor theatres, and bandshells, where one may study if one is taking a course in music or drama, dancing, or anything else which might require this type of setting. Whatever your course of study, there is an area that is quite suitable for your particular interest. In this way, one can move from the indoor classroom to the outdoor area with no problems, whatsoever.

Here, on the other side of life, we are not concerned with day and night, as you are there on Earth. Our day never ends. Therefore, classes are always in progress and one may attend when one wishes to do so. And, one has much time for leisure activities. At The University we have concert halls, and theatres, art galleries, sports fields, and a center for every kind of leisure activity that you can think of, perhaps, even more. There is something going on at every conceivable level so that no matter what your interest may be, from the simplest forms of music, to grand opera; from a one-act play to the most serious types of drama; from spectator sports to those in which one may participate, it is all here.

There are special areas for the young people and for the small children. No one can ever say, "I have nothing to do." Although, if one wishes to do nothing that is acceptable. Doing nothing can be very pleasant at times, and we do not have to be busy every moment. As long as we understand what it is we have been assigned to do and we work at these tasks, we are on our own, more or less. Of course, reports are kept on our progress with our assigned tasks, but here, again, one moves at a pace which is comfortable for that particular individual. Here on the other side of life, progress is a personal matter. There are those, however, who would become lazy, at times, and not wish to move at all, as far as their assigned tasks are concerned. When this happens, the individual is taken aside by the counselor assigned to him and is gently reminded that no work means no progress, and that there are many interesting things awaiting the individual as he completes each task. This is usually all that is required to get the individual back in motion again. If, for some reason, we find one who will not listen and continues to make no progress, that individual is sent to another area and there must work his way back up to the level he had been on previously. This usually works wonders, and it is not long before an individual is back and eager to move on.

Chapter **XIII**
OTHER TIMES, OTHER PLACES

Have you longed to travel to distant lands, but never been able to do so? If you have reached a state of evolution while you are on Earth that provides you with the key to The Garden, and gains entry, for you, to the higher planes, here on the other side of life, you may travel anywhere you wish. Some of us here travel in connection with our studies at The University. We who are interested in ancient history, or in the study of one particular country or one particular area, are allowed to travel to that country or place to learn more of these places than we could from books and lectures. In this way, we can study first-hand, the customs, the language, the art, music and everything else there is to know about a particular country.

I have always been interested in England, and in India, and, of course, in Arabia. When I crossed over to life here on the other side, I was very pleased to find that I could travel to these countries at will and learn more about them than would ever have been possible while I was on the Earth plane. I have studied these countries from their very beginnings to the present time, and I have seen what the future holds for them also.

You cannot imagine what it is like to return to some long-forgotten place in time and see exactly the way things were at that time. There are many things which history books do not tell you, and that is understandable, for there are many things which took place which were never recorded. And, some of the history which was recorded was not written exactly as it happened, but rather as it was seen by a human being, and the truth is often distorted. I have seen life as it actually happened at whatever point in time I wished to return to. You cannot know how exciting this can be.

It is interesting to note how things change over the years. Of course, there are changes in costume, in hair styles, in laws. But, over the course of time there are also changes in physical structure of the individuals who live in a particular country. There are changes in customs, in social graces, in living habits and even changes in the language which is spoken in that particular country. Perhaps you are thinking that this is not new information, as far as you are concerned. But, think how exciting it would be for you to actually see all these changes taking place. In one's lifetime on Earth one would perhaps see a few changes, but nothing can compare to what we can see from this side of the veil.

India today is overpopulated, and there is much need there for improvement in living conditions. But, it was not always so. There was a time when India was a very splendid country, and even those who were not of royal ancestry were not so poor that they did not have a decent and respectable way of life. There were irrigation systems which created lush gardens, and there was plenty to eat for all. People worked together, and those who had more shared with those who had less so that there was a balance to the living there. It is said that "Time changes all things". This is not so, for it is *man* who changes all things. And it is man who can take what is good and turn it around to his advantage and to the disadvantage of many. I have also seen this.

In getting the overall picture of a certain country or of a certain civilization, one can then see, perhaps, why certain things happened as they did and what can be done to prevent these same things from happening again, if they were undesirable, and, if they were caused by man. There are changes which God has caused for one reason or another, but, here, again, drastic changes which God makes are usually necessary because of something man has or has not done. However, if one understands why God made these changes, they, also, can be prevented from happening again.

As we learn about other cultures, other countries, other areas of civilization, we then are more equipped to handle our work when it comes to teaching and guiding those of you who are still on the Earth plane. We try to lead you in paths which will be pleasing to God and, therefore, unwanted, unpleasant, changes are unnecessary. Unfortunately, since most of you are unaware that we are here, and do not listen, we are not always successful in our attempts, and disasters do strike.

We can also, if we desire to do so, project ourselves into the future and see what is in store for a particular country, or a particular race of people. This can be very enlightening and, here again, we use the knowledge we obtain to try to make those of you who are on Earth aware of the things which may not be very pleasant, so that you can start to alter your lives and, thus, alter your future. If you would only listen!

Some of us study these countries to which we travel in order that we might help someone on Earth to write more accurate history books. There are those with whom we can work, who have opened themselves up to us that we may write through them. The one to whom I am dictating this particular book is such a person. She has been chosen to write these lessons that you may understand how to improve your life, now, so that you may enter through The Garden Gate when you cross over to the other side of life. Others have been chosen to write music, books on history, books on health, and just about every subject imaginable. I say that these writers have been chosen to do this work, however, some who are chosen do not wish to do this, and we never force ourselves upon them. At times, it is difficult to find a medium who is willing to do our work. Therefore, we are most grateful to those who take the time to work with us.

Those who write for us, books, poetry, music, whatever it is they have been chosen to do, need never worry about an outlet for their material, for we will see that all the details are taken care of when the time comes. Of what importance would a book be if it were never published so that others could read and learn from it? What good is music that no one will hear? We take care of all the arrangements to be sure that there is a place for the work which we have dictated.

I have gone into an explanation of these things so that you may see that even though travel is a pleasure here, for us, we also use these trips which we take to help others, whenever we find the opportunity to do so. In our lives here, we are always striving to do something for someone else, whether that someone be here in spirit or back on Earth. That is what life is all about.

Chapter XIV
LEISURE TIME

It is time now to tell you what we do with our leisure time. It is not always necessary for us to be studying, teaching, striving to grow and progress. We have much time when we can do whatever it is we are inclined to do for our own enjoyment. I, for one, like to stroll leisurely through the gardens which abound here. I have mentioned several times "The Garden" through which some enter this plane of life, however, there are other gardens here which are for the use of all those who have begun to progress and to find their way. The Garden which I have spoken of before, is a very special one and there is no comparison between that one and the others which are found here, although they are all very beautiful. The Garden has a special feeling for it is there that one first feels the presence of God as one enters this side of life and even I cannot describe the feeling that permeates every flower and tree, bird and animal and even the very air in The Garden.

In the other gardens one feels God's love and presence, also, but because we are surrounded by it at all times here on the other side of life, it is not so powerful as the feeling that one received when first entering by The Garden. I am sure that you have all attended parties at one time or another and had a very enjoyable time. The atmosphere was pleasant and the feeling of friendship and love was there. Have you ever attended a party that was given in your honor? The same friends were there, the same refreshments were served, but something was different. There was a different feeling in the air . . . this was something special, something that showed you how much you were loved and appreciated by your friends. This is the difference between The Garden and the many other gardens which we have here.

God has given us, here on this plane, so much beauty that it goes beyond description, and I can only try to tell you of some of the things that I see. As I stroll through the gardens, the music of the birds fills the air, but it is such a beautiful *blending* of sound, that one is never so conscious of it that one loses sight of all the *other* beauty that is here. Soft breezes move the trees and the flowers, and one is never sure whether the music comes from these or from the birds, it is all blended together so well. There are flowers here which no mortal eye has seen. Those of you who are aware of this plane of existence, and who can see beyond the limitations of the human eye, have, perhaps, visualized these flowers and the colors. However, if I were to say to most of you "red, orange, yellow, green, blue, violet", you would understand these colors and, perhaps, you could also visualize the many different shades that come from blending and shadings of these. You cannot, however, imagine colors which you have never seen and here we have color that your eye could not perceive even though it were shown to you.

Form and shape is also different here. There are flowers which defy description. You see roses, daffodils, tulips, but we have here thousands of flowers which you have never seen, each one lovelier than the one before it and yet, they are all growing so that they blend with and complement each other and give joy to the beholder. Fragrance fills the air. One cannot separate one fragrance from another, they are so skillfully blended. Yet, one is aware of each one, and, at the same time, of the whole.

Have you seen a butterfly? Beauty on the wing. Here, they are breathtakingly beautiful. Their sizes range from tiny creatures of vivid color who seem to be part of the flowers, to those whose wings are so large that they seem to be flowers floating through the air.

We are allowed to pick the flowers here, if we wish to do so, but one rarely does for there is so much beauty here that one does not need to pick a few flowers to take some of the

66

beauty away with him. One need only look about, and the beauty is there.

I enjoy these walks through the gardens. I find that I am able to understand many things that I need to understand as I go through life here, as I walk quietly through the gardens. The peace that fills the air, the beauty around me, all help me to understand more easily the lessons I have to learn and, also to understand more about helping those whom I have been assigned to help here in spirit and back on the earth plane.

Walking along through the gardens one may come upon a stream or a pool of crystal clear water. I like to sit beside one pool, in particular, which has a little waterfall tumbling down into it, and it is here that I do much of my thinking and it is here that I have chosen to sit when I gather my thoughts together for these lessons I have given you.

The creatures who live in the gardens are friendly, and as I sit and relax and do my thinking, they come up to me and allow me to pet them. There are some who seem to wait for me to come for they are always here when I stroll down the pathway to the little pool. What joy there is to see how all of nature can live together peacefully. It is sad that you on Earth cannot enjoy this relationship also, but, if man cannot live peacefully with man, how, then, can he be expected to live peacefully with the other creatures on Earth?

As I have said, I, personally, enjoy the gardens in my leisure moments. However, one does not have to walk through the gardens to enjoy beauty. There is beauty and peace everywhere you go. Green fields, wild flowers, beautiful trees, and everywhere the feeling of peace and contentment. Music is heard, and yet one is never so conscious of it that it becomes annoying. On the contrary, it blends in so easily and nicely with the surroundings and with the sounds of the breeze, that, at times, one wonders if he really heard it at all. Peace; everywhere there is peace and love.

The sun is warm on us, and I cannot describe to you the feeling that one gets from this light. For, it is The Light, the light of the *Son,* the Christ Light which shines so brightly here. It nourishes us and fills us with love and peace and we, in turn, reflect this light to others, not only here, but back to you on Earth, also. Most of you are not aware that we do this, but those of you who are, understand, for you can feel some of the joy and love that we feel here as we are bathed in this light.

If one wishes to use his leisure time in other ways, there are many activities going on here which one can attend, or take part in. There are sports, concerts, shows, exhibits, friendly gatherings, picnics, dances. Whatever you might be interested in is available to you, for there will be many who share that interest. There is always something pleasant to do, and, if none of these fit your mood, you can just *sit* and enjoy doing nothing. It is your choice.

Chapter **XV**
SPEAK, AND I WILL UNDERSTAND

One of the most beautiful and interesting things about being here, on the other side of life, is the fact that we can communicate with whomever we choose, without worrying about language barriers. You have heard the expression "It's all Greek to me"? Well here it is Greek, Polish, Italian, French, Arabic or whatever language is being spoken. I say spoken, however, we do not speak as you do, we speak to each other through mental communication. Therefore, when a person of one nationality speaks his native language those of other nationalities can understand it perfectly for as we receive the message, it is translated into language which we can all understand. This is really great for if there were language barriers here, there would be no harmony. If it were difficult to communicate with one another, after a time, perhaps, one would just give up trying and stay with those who spoke the same language as he.

This is not only true of communication here on the other side of life, but also true of communication between those of us in spirit and those of you who are still on Earth.

If you are an individual who is aware of your spirit guides and you can communicate with them easily, you probably have never given a thought to how this works. Are you aware of who your guides are? Are some of them, perhaps from India, or Germany? Do you have a guide who is an American Indian, or perhaps a Chinese scholar? Have you never wondered how it is that they can speak with you and that you can understand what it is they say to you. They have not learned the English language merely to be able to communicate with you. They speak in their own language and it is transformed into the language that you can understand as it passes from one mind to the other.

There is another interesting aspect to this communication system. If a group of mediums, or people who are receptive to spirit communication are gathered together and someone in spirit communicates with them, several of the people present may pick up the thought at the same time and even though they present the message in slightly different variations, each one understands the message clearly. The reason for the variance in delivery of the message is that each one has received the communication in the language he understands and in a way that he can understand it best.

For example: Someone has a question concerning a change in their place of employment. There are three mediums present. "Is it wise for me to make a change in my place of employment at this time and seek another job?" One answer may be "Sit tight," another "This is not the time", and a third, "There is a change in your future, soon." There are three answers with different wording and yet only one answer was given by the spirit messenger. Each medium picks up the message in his or her own way and yet, all three of them are correct.

If you have ever been to a medium for a reading, you may have noted a slight change of voice, or a different way of speaking, or a change in mannerism as the medium spoke to you. Sometimes, rather than the medium just relaying the message which spirit gives, spirit actually uses the medium's voice box and does the talking. The medium does not have to be in a trance for this to happen, only to step aside and let spirit use them. It is very interesting to those of you who have not seen this before, to sit through a reading and wonder how this is possible. It is all very easy, if one opens himself up and begins to work with us. I will tell you more of this later, how to open up, how to develop, but we will get back to how one communicates here, on the other side of life, at this time.

Because there are really no language barriers here, one would suppose that it is not necessary to learn other languages. This is not so. It is important to learn and to preserve the knowledge of all languages for, we act as teachers and tutors to those of you who are on Earth. Many of us are assigned to help those of you who are having trouble with languages, whether it be a language you have decided to study, or your own native tongue. Most of you are not aware of the help you receive from us, but, nevertheless, we do help, whenever we can.

We also help in situations where someone who speaks a language which is foreign to the listener is having a difficult time trying to make that person understand what is needed, or wanted. Suddenly, the listener has a feeling that he knows what is being said, although he still has no more knowledge of the language than he did a moment before. We are working with him. We have translated the unknown language into a thought which the other person can understand. It is not necessarily done word for word, but the important meaning of the message is given.

I, myself, am fascinated by languages. I have learned many. I am proficient in Arabic, German, Hindustani and French, and I am interested in the language of the American Indians, as spoken by the different tribes. Latin, also, is one which I am working on, in order that I may understand more of this now little used, but once important language.

One of the things that interests me as far as the language of the American Indian is concerned, is not only the spoken word, but the way the language is expressed through the movement of the hands, the body. It is as though the voice, the body are all one with nature and the Universe.

Do not think that because we communicate on a mental level here that we are always intruding on another's privacy. We would not do that here, any more than we would interfere with you who are on Earth. We communicate with each other easily, but we are not tuned in to each other constantly,

71

for then we would have no privacy, and we would be very confused with thoughts bombarding us from all sides, at all times. It works the same here as it does there with you. If we wish to speak with someone we contact them mentally. If they do not wish to be bothered, it is as though no one has answered the phone when we called, and we do not pressure them. If there is a matter of great importance which must be discussed or given to them, they can feel this and then they will be receptive to our thoughts.

Trying to communicate with some of you there on Earth is another story! Sometimes it is very important that you be made aware of some particular situation, and we must keep trying, as long as we possibly can to help you to see, to understand. Most times we are unsuccessful, as people are not aware of us, and then they bumble along through situations which could have been avoided if they had been aware of our help. Have you tried listening lately? We are always here.

Chapter **XVI**
TRANSITION WITHOUT TRAUMA

There comes a time when one who has passed on to the other side of life must be ready to help those who come over because of some disaster which has taken place on Earth. You, there on the earth plane, have emergency systems for fire, floods, earthquakes, accidents. We, here on the other side of life, also have groups ready to assist in times of emergency. Not only do we try to reach those of you who are caught in the disaster and give you guidance, we must also be ready to receive those who "die" (as you would say) because of some terrible thing that has happened. I am not speaking now of individual deaths, but of those times when a great many people are involved: air crashes, train accidents, and all the terrible disasters that nature can perform. We must be ready, here, to help those who cross over in the event of such disasters. These things can be very traumatic, if one is not prepared to understand what awaits one here on the other side of life.

There, on Earth, policemen, firemen, doctors and others rush quickly to the aid of the injured and those in need. We, here, also rush to the aid of those who need us, but in this case it is to the aid of those who have crossed over because of some disaster. You can imagine the confusion as many enter here at one time, bewildered, lost, unaware, perhaps, that they have even left the physical body behind. We must be ready to try to help them find their way, to help them to understand what it is that has happened to them and to try to help them adjust to the change that has taken place so suddenly.

We have groups of entities here who are especially prepared to help those who come over in this manner. Many of these who are in our "emergency squads" are familiar with the trauma as they had passed over in the same manner at one time.

You realize, of course, that once one crosses over, there is no pain, for all that is left behind with the physical body. However, there is confusion. Some wander about searching for a familiar face, or a member of the family. Some wander about aimlessly not knowing where they are, or even where they had been before the disaster which brought them here. It is a terrible shock to most of them.

In the event of individual crossings it is often difficult for us to reach the one who has just come over to this side of life, but when you have crowds of new arrivals, each one more confused than the one before him, it is a very trying time for us. We have to console, to show the way, to try to make each individual understand where he is and what has happened to him. Those who have been prepared for some sort of life after death are more easily reached and as they become aware, they are led to other areas, away from the confusion that is taking place at the point at which the new arrivals have entered.

Most times, it takes a great deal of time to get everyone adjusted and aware of their surroundings. It is very difficult to reach some of them. As each becomes aware he is then ready to move on to receive further instruction and become more adjusted to his new home. With those who have difficulty understanding that there is something more than limbo waiting for them, we work on a one-to-one basis until such time as they are ready to move on.

Even though there are no physical injuries to contend with, no pain, once the physical body has been left behind, we are as careful and considerate of those who pass over as you are of those who are taken to hospitals to be treated for burns or injuries. And, as you are kind and considerate to those who have lost members of their family, we, here, are also as considerate to those who have left their family behind. For, even though "death" happens all the time, it is never so terrible and frightening to those who are left behind, nor to those who have crossed over, as when it happens to a great number at one time.

One begins to wonder why such disasters are necessary. Why so many must leave the Earth plane at one time is difficult to comprehend. I wish that I could give you an answer. But, unfortunately, it is only God who knows the answer. We, here, do not question and ask "Why?", we only do our work, as we have been prepared to do it, to help those who come to us at times like these.

Once each individual becomes aware of what awaits him here, he then moves along, just as any other individual who enters in a more orderly fashion.

Much of the confusion that is caused when a great number cross over at the same time, is brought on by the fact that these individuals can see and hear the confusion that is still going on below them, on the Earth plane, and many are not aware that they have left the body and, so, they run around trying to help, trying to find lost possessions, or lost loved ones. You, on Earth only see what is happening there on your plane, at the time of a disaster, but we can see your side and also see what we have to take care of here. It is a very difficult time for us, as it is for you.

Here, again, if one is prepared and understands more about what happens when the physical body is left behind, and one becomes spirit, much of this trauma can be averted whether one crosses over peacefully in one's sleep or whether one has a very traumatic "death". Remember, it is up to you. Knowing that there is help for you and being aware that there is more to life than just what you have there on Earth can make all the difference in how you adjust when you arrive over here. Hopefully, those of you who are reading this book will understand more of what is necessary to help you make the change when it is time for you to cross over to the other side of life. For, it should be no more than the experience of moving from one familiar home to a new one, which you have heard about, and, perhaps, imagined but have not yet seen. New neighbors, new surroundings, new things to do and see . . . why should that be frightening? If you think of it this way, you will not be frightened when you cross over, nor will you be unaware that there are good things awaiting you, on the other side of life.

Yes, there will be loved ones left behind, friends, places we are familiar with, but is this not true of any move that takes you a distance from the place you have lived in for some time? You can see your friends, your family, and, if you have helped them to understand that life does not end with the death of the physical body, they, too, can communicate with you and know that you are still close to them. And this is the way that God meant it to be.

If you think about it, there are two sides to nearly everything that you see. Most objects have a front and a back, a top and a bottom, a right and a left, or an inside and an outside. There are two sides to every coin, and, it is said that there are two sides to every story.

Remember this, also. There are two sides to your life; the one in the physical body and the one which continues when you become spirit and are no longer encumbered by that physical body . . . The Other Side of Life.

Chapter **XVII**
THE GIFT

Now we move on to more pleasant things. Would you like to know more about developing the wonderful gift that God has given to you? Yes, you have been given many gifts, but I speak of the finest gift of all, the ability to communicate with those who are pure spirit; those who are beyond the sight of the physical eye and beyond the sound of the physical ear. You all have this gift. What you do with it, however, is up to you.

If someone were to walk up to you and say, "I have a free gift for you. It costs you nothing, and though you cannot see it, the more you use it the more valuable it becomes." What would you do? Would you accept his offer, or turn your back and walk away mumbling about the "strange" person who made the offer to you? The gift is free, and it is yours, all you have to do is to acknowledge it and begin to use it. Once you have accepted the fact that there is "something there" and you begin to make use of it, you will wonder why you have never been interested in using this gift before this time.

There is nothing "spooky" or "weird" about those who do communicate with spirit, as they go about their daily lives. They are involved in a most natural part of daily living, that is: communication with entities who can guide and teach and help in all areas of life.

Communication with the other side of life is as easy as the process of thinking. Once you become aware that we are here to help you, all you have to do is think and we can offer you help and guidance in all areas of your life. Learn to talk to us mentally or, if you prefer, verbally and learn to listen and to feel and you will be shown the way. It takes a little practice before one begins to understand how the answers and the guidance come through, but once you get the "feeling" of how it works, you are on the way.

One does not have to become a medium or a prophet because one communicates with spirit. One may use this at any time for the betterment of his own life. Mediums are important, as they can communicate with us and pass on messages to those who are not aware that they, themselves, can do this. However, each individual should learn to develop his own abilities to communicate with us so that the lines of communication may be used at any time, without the need to consult a medium. Communication with spirit should be thought of as talking with friends, for that is exactly what we are, your friends. We are here to help you and while each of us is not all-knowing, each individual's own guides will obtain information or help necessary for that particular person.

"What are guides?" you ask. To each individual on the Earth plane there are assigned several entities in spirit to guide, teach and to help that person in all areas of his life. Also, there are those in spirit who become attached to you for some reason or other and they, also, are called your guides. Guides are not necessarily someone you knew when they were on the Earth plane although occasionally someone who had been close to you on Earth will be allowed to guide you, for a time, when they are in spirit. Guides come and go, just as friends and acquaintances do there on Earth. As you progress and grow and move on to higher levels of understanding and spiritual growth, your guides change. Also, if you do not grow, but remain at the level which you have been on for some time, your guides will change, for as they progress and grow, they move on to other things. One would not expect to have a nursery school teacher for a high school class, nor a high school teacher for a nursery class.

As guides, we are not here to tell you which way to turn and what moves to make every second of your life, but we are available to help you with important decisions, problems which are a burden to you and we also guide you to those

78

people or places where you can develop into the person you should be, both on the material plane and on the spiritual plane.

Once you get into working with spirit and having us work with you, it may cause you to understand that we have been helping you all along the way, even though you were not even aware of our existence. How many times have you just had a "feeling" that something was right for you, or wrong for you, and, therefore, did not get yourself involved in something that would have been detrimental or harmful to you? Have you ever been kept from going somewhere or doing something and later found that had you gone something dreadful would have happened to you? "Luck", you say. Only in the sense that you were "lucky" to have had us around at the time, watching out for you. Think about your life up to this point, and you will, undoubtedly, find many instances of help given to you by spirit.

God has made us his messengers, his teachers, his physicians, and we have been assigned to help those who are still in the physical body, that they may have a better life. It is not important to you that you know us by name, only that you know us. The most difficult part of opening the lines of communication will be when you try to determine which thought is your own and which is coming from the other side of life. True, some people do hear "other voices", but most often the answers you seek, or the guidance you receive will come through to you as your own thought, but the more you develop your awareness of us and the more you work with us, the easier it will be to distinguish between your own thoughts and our communications with you. At times, you won't hear anything but you may get a feeling about something, and, if you act on that feeling, you will find that all will be well. Calling this feeling intuition, or a hunch is fine, but when you begin to acknowledge that the guidance came from spirit and you say "thank you", new doors begin to open up in your life.

I am sure that you have all heard stories about evil spirits, occult happenings that have been very harmful or dangerous to someone, and possession. Yes, these things exist, and you must be aware that they do; however, they need never concern you. Are there not people on Earth who would do harm, who would create danger for another human being or possess them to the extent that they actually live another person's life for them, not allowing them to think or do for themselves? You are aware that such things exist on the Earth plane, but you try to live your life in such a way that these things do not touch you. So it is, in dealing with the world of spirit. When you first begin to open yourself up to communicating with us, just "know" that you are dealing with God's highest forces and that you would not *allow* any of the lower forces to interfere in your life, and you will be protected by those in spirit whose task it is to help you to progress, spiritually.

If you should feel uncomfortable, in the beginning, and wish to protect yourself further, you need only ask God to watch over you and ask him to allow only those of the highest order to come into your life. Or, when you are about to begin your communications, recite the Lord's Prayer, or some other prayer which appeals to you.

You may, also, surround yourself, from time to time, with the Pure White Light of Christ. This is easily done. You may imagine that you are under a shower and, rather than water, you are being bathed in a brilliant white light, which covers you and protects you. Or, you might like to imagine that you are wrapped in a cocoon of this pure white light.

Some people who begin to get involved with spirit communication look for the excitement of making tables move, walls knock and playing with ouija boards. DON'T DO THIS! When you begin to play with these things, you are opening yourself up to the lower spirit world. And, once you associate with them, it is difficult to get rid of them. It is like joining a street gang to get a little excitement in your life.

They may let you join, but you will have difficulty in trying to drop your membership with the group.

If you begin correctly and only correspond with those of the highest order, they will see that you are protected at all times, and you will find plenty of excitement once you begin to work with us. Just opening up the lines of communication with us is excitement in itself. And, as you see the many ways in which we work with you, you will understand just how great communication can be between your world and ours.

Chapter XVIII
SEANCE

Have you ever been to a Seance? My, that's another "spooky" word, isn't it? You have probably been misinformed about this type of communication with spirit, also. There is nothing "spooky" about it.

To begin with, the word seance has been misused, as has the seance itself. You have probably read about, or seen motion pictures about seances where articles are flying through the air, and voices are heard and mysterious white figures float about. In most cases these have been "rigged" to give the person attending the seance exactly what he or she came for, *a show.* Or, you heard that Mrs. Riches attended a seance to speak to her deceased husband in order to find out where he put his last will. If she could find that one and destroy it, she would still be "in the money", by presenting the previous one. Why should this person think that a man who wouldn't speak to her while he was living is going to speak to her now that he has passed on to the other side of life?

A seance is supposed to be a place of learning, a classroom. Again, one should ask to deal only with the spirits of the highest order when attending or conducting a seance. Therefore, it is wise to know the reputation of the medium who is in charge of the seance which you might plan to attend. If one wishes to learn more about spirit communication for the betterment of his own life, or would like to develop as a medium, the place to go is a seance.

The seance is not conducted for the purpose of getting in touch with relatives or friends who have passed on, although, occasionally, a relative or friend may be allowed to come through to speak with someone at the seance, if it is important for that particular person, or that particular spirit.

You who are still on the Earth plane think that there is nothing else for your loved ones to do but to sit and wait until you decide to communicate with them. Rarely is this the case. Most of us here are very busy and we have many tasks to perform and lessons to learn, as I have explained to you. Your loved ones may be on a higher plane, where it is difficult for them to come down to your level, unless it is extremely important that they do this. If it is necessary, they will come to you without your calling for them.

When you become part of a group conducting a seance, if you are there simply to satisfy your curiosity, that is all right, the first time. Or, perhaps, even a second time. However, you will probably find that very soon you are unable to make the classes for one reason or another and soon do not go at all. This is our doing. We are very selective, and we choose very carefully those with whom we wish to work. We have much to teach those who are sincere, but we have not time to waste on those who come only out of idle curiosity.

Most of you believe that anything that has to do with spirit communication has to be very somber. This is not so. We, too, like a good laugh once in a while, and there will be times at a seance when everyone has a chance to really laugh, but whether the seance is filled with laughter or takes on a more sedate atmosphere, there is always the feeling of upliftment and joy, during and after the meeting. After all, it is a gathering of friends.

Occasionally, some troubled spirit may be allowed to come through at a seance. I say "troubled" not "evil". There are those who do need help, and if they are allowed to come through, it is to receive help from those who attend the seance, as they probably can reach this troubled spirit much more easily than we can. Many times, it just takes that little bit of contact with your side of life to help someone over here adjust to their new life.

We have many lessons to teach. Some of them are aimed at the spiritual side of your life, but others are not. We can teach on any subject and the only thing that governs the type of lesson taught, is the type of group. One group may be taught only one or two subjects, and other groups may have more subjects given to them. It all depends on the individuals involved in that particular group.

It is best for those who are not familiar with working with the spirit world to begin to open up their own awareness under the direction of a qualified teacher. There are many who say that they will show you the way to do this and, yet, they know little about it. Some have, perhaps, read up on this and others may have experienced it, but still are not qualified to show others the way. Most of you will find that if you desire, *sincerely,* to work with us, we will help you even before you become aware that we are able to do this. When you begin to feel a desire to learn more about us and how to communicate with us, we will direct you to the proper classes, teachers, whatever is necessary for your spiritual growth. However, do not overlook the word "sincerely" which I have used above. If you are merely interested in fun and games, don't look to us for help. Go wherever you choose. We won't be paying much attention to you until we know that the spiritual spark in you has been flamed and you do "sincerely" wish to learn more.

When that particular moment comes, we will direct you so that you are able to open up your awareness and develop your abilities. If you are in classes which are not suitable for your particular needs, we will see to it that you are unable to continue these classes, and we will direct you to something more suitable. If you are not studying, but wish to do so, we will direct you to people and places where you may learn more of what you are seeking. We will give you books to read. (No, they won't materialize out of thin air, but we will see that they are given to you or that you are directed to a particular book which is right for you.)

You will find it most interesting, as you begin to become more aware of how spirit communication works, and you will enjoy the many new friends and acquaintances you will

84

meet as you are directed along the path to spiritual growth. I know, as you read this, that some of you are thinking that you are going to be led around by a ring in your nose. This is not so, for you can, at any time, do exactly as you please. We direct and guide you, we do not *force* you. You always have free will.

As you progress along the pathway of spiritual growth, you will begin to understand more about how God works through the spirit forces. You might think that we were "taking over" since I am always talking about "We, We, We,". It is God who directs us, and it is His work which we do when we work with you. We are instruments and channels for God's work to reach you who are still on the Earth plane, just as you who are developing your abilities will become channels for God's work, also, by opening yourself up to do healing, teaching, mediumship, or just by becoming more spiritually attuned so that you are a light for others as you go through life.

In time, you will, perhaps, be directed to a seance, a classroom of higher learning. As you continue to meet with your particular group, you will find that you become more and more attuned to working with us, as each session is ended. You will find that there is a difference in your ability to communicate with us. You will find, also, that you begin to become a more beautiful human being for the spirit that is within you is being nourished by the lessons you are receiving and by your reaching out for more and more spiritual development.

You will find, also, that those who are involved in the seance are some of the most beautiful individuals you have ever met, for we direct only those who have reached a certain stage of spiritual growth to these seances, and there is such a strong feeling of love between those who are involved, that a feeling of peace fills the whole room wherever these people gather for their classroom work.

It is, indeed, unfortunate that so much has been done to promote Spiritualism as being something evil, or phony.

Certainly some of you on the Earth plane have had bad experiences with spirit communication, only because you were not ready to do this, and, also, because you were not taught the proper way to go about this. As with everything else in life, there is a right way and a wrong way. Because you have heard of some bad experiences, does that mean that you should stay away from something that would be very beneficial to your life? Electricity is very helpful to you on Earth, in many ways, and, yet, if it is not used properly, it can shock you. An electrical shock can be so mild that you think nothing of it or so severe that it can cause death. I am sure you have heard many stories of such deaths, or injuries, and you still use electricity in your everyday life. All you have to remember is that it must be used *wisely, carefully.* People drown every day in swimming or boating accidents. You still use your bathtub and your swimming pool, don't you?

Why, then, do you shy away from the thought that you could communicate with those who have passed on, those on the other side of life? All you have to remember is that if you follow the rules, and do not abuse this gift of communication, you will run into no problems. As usual, it is those who think they know everything, and yet know nothing who will find themselves in trouble, for they will, most likely, plunge into some form of spirit communication without first having some understanding of how and why it works. Most will want to "see" something happening or they will not believe that there is anything going on at all. This is when you will hear stories of poltergeist and other phenomenon, of "evil" spirits causing problems.

The reason it is so easy to make something happen when you want to see quick results of your attempts at spirit communication, is that the lower forces are always ready to oblige you with a show. They are not always "evil" but, rather, so little evolved spiritually, that they do not care what it is they do, as long as someone is aware of their presence. Once the door is opened by someone on Earth to allow these low forces to come in, it is very difficult to rid yourself of them.

Begin with a sincere desire to work with only the highest forces. Talk with your guides, either verbally, or mentally. They are always ready to be of service to you. You may not be able to discern their presence, at first, but as time goes on, you will be aware that they are working with you. Use this precious gift that God has given you, and your life will be enriched.

Conclusion

The time has come for me to move on. There are others with whom I must work, not only for their progression, but also for mine. In giving you the lessons and the information which I have set forth here in this book, I have tried to give you the knowledge that will create a desire within you to set your feet upon the path of spiritual growth. If I have started you thinking and wondering and wishing to know more, that is good. For that is how one begins. Once you have made the beginning, you will find that more and more knowledge and understanding will come to you as you progress.

It has been very interesting for me, preparing these lessons for you. In teaching, one has to be very careful that the lessons are not too long, nor too difficult, in order that those for whom they are intended do not grow weary. When students grow weary, information falls on deaf ears and nothing is gained.

Consider yourself fortunate for you have been directed to this book, to this knowledge. Make good use of it and see how enriched your life will be, how much more interesting.

Begin now to set your feet upon the pathway to spiritual growth and understanding, so that when it is time for you to make the transition, you may enter through The Garden, to the Other Side of Life.